BOUNDARY LEADERS
Leadership Skills for People of Faith

Gary Gunderson

Fortress Press
Minneapolis

BOUNDARY LEADERS
Leadership Skills for People of Faith

Cover image: © Photodisc
Cover design: Marti Naughton
Author photo: Kay Hinton © Emory University Photography
Interior design: James Korsmo

Library of Congress Cataloging-in-Publication Data

Gunderson, Gary.
  Boundary leaders : leadership skills for people of faith / Gary Gunderson.
    p. cm.
  ISBN 0-8006-3194-3 (alk. paper)
  1. Church work. 2. Christian leadership. 3. Church and social problems. I.
  Title.
  BV4400.G86 2004
  253—dc22
                                                                2004012831

The paper used in this publication meets the minimum requirements of
American National Standard for Information Sciences — Permanence of
Paper for Printed Library Materials, ANSI Z329.48-1984.

Manufactured in the U.S.A.

08   07   06   05   04   1   2   3   4   5   6   7   8   9   10

Contents

Preface

In a time of almost infinite capacity for fear I am writing of hope. In a time obsessed by security I recommend the insecurity of the complex and contested space I call the boundary zones. At a time when so many feel powerless, I am describing the webs of relationships that are transforming our world in hopeful ways. I am either delusional or onto something that will be very good news to you.

One clue that I may not be delusional is that this book has not grown from my imagination, but from the last three decades of being with thousands of boundary leaders whose pattern of life and leadership I describe here. The idea of boundary leadership hasn't come from the wealthy and wonderful on TV. Rather, I have found it among those working in the heart of racism, AIDS, intractable public health catastrophes and grinding poverty. This is exactly where the life and leadership I see in boundary leaders is more evident. This is leadership for deep and stormy water; a way to live with integrity amid things that can barely be named. This is faith that matters because it makes possible a life that matters.

> **This is leadership for deep and stormy water.**

If you picked up a book with this title, it may be that you are tired of playing inside the lines of old strategies that make us complicit with despair. If so, come along with me into the boundary zones. You'll find a new name and a way of leading that offers serious hope for you, and for the world we share. It might feel like waking up from one of those very depressing and confusing dreams adults are prone to. It's time. So, come this way.

Gary Gunderson

1

Come This Way

I have not even one family in my parish that has so much as one brick in their home, they are so poor. Our community health clinic has been replaced by an AIDS center. When the mother leading our AIDS care team was diagnosed with AIDS herself, her husband threw her out of the house and away from her children. Her birth family would not take her back, so in a month she died in a box-shelter on the church grounds."

This is AIDS in Africa: mothers dying in boxes. Petros, a Lutheran pastor, knew that I knew many thousands of women are dying in such boxes in many thousands of villages. His soft strong voice paused, his eyes met mine. "So, Gary, what word would you have for me?"

The seven other students in my religion seminar in Cape Town joined our silence. They all could have told the same story with accents from Zimbabwe, Indonesia, Namibia, Uganda. They knew I had no word for Petros or for them that would make the catastrophe of AIDS less devastating.

Petros was not asking how to run his church or for tips on how improve his community health program. He was asking a question from the deep mystery of our time, caught between the astonishing capacities of our technical systems and the banal suffering of mothers in boxes. Not many people in my city wake up knowing they will face the same scale of challenges of faith and action as Petros, but the questions are just as profound.

How am I to live? What do I do? What word do I have for Petros? His question echoes many fundamental questions about what it is possible to hope for.

What is possible to ask of himself, as father, pastor, community leader, Christian, citizen?

What is possible to ask of his congregation, its strengths, liabilities, and possibilities?

What is possible to ask of his community in all its complexity?

What is possible to ask of his denomination, his religious connectional system(s)?

What is possible to ask of his government and, can we say, intergovernmental complex?

What is possible to ask of his human connections that extend even to Atlanta?

What is possible to ask of his teachers (and their teachers)?

Petros was not posing questions that might be interesting to consider. These are all alive and burning in the eyes of those he sees in his daily walk. So it is with us, too.

Don't Just Stand There—Lead!

A great amount of the thinking of those known as scholars is recreational and, increasingly, entrepreneurial. That is, we think about things that entertain us and those things we imagine we can be paid to think about. I do not think the situation is much different in our pulpits. We run our congregations toward those things that entertain our members and might attract others. A great deal of our teaching is framed by topics that we like to teach and that will make our stream of students, and those who might pay them someday, happy. In normal times—times when things are going well enough—that is acceptable behavior and is, at worst, harmless. These are not normal times. Indeed, the complex of disorienting crises made nearly impossible to think about by the scale and multiplicity of HIV/AIDS and the other crucial disparities I will address in these pages marks a generational shift. Not only are our various civic and religious structures and systems in fundamental disarray, but our conceptual frameworks are shattered too. In such a time the first question is not "What is wrong?" but "What do we have to work with?" That is, what are our assets? What word do we have for one another?

> **I know that Petros's church member was a sister of mine whose ugly death is a scandal that involves me too.**

This book grows out of my search for that word. Silence before this unholy horror may be more appropriate, but we must speak to one another and offer what we can. Thus, my word.

I am trying to follow Jesus as best a middle-class white male can, which is to say, not very well. I could add other adjectives for myself, but none would make mine sound anything remotely like the lifestyle of the first-century itinerant carpenter whose example I choose to emulate. But even cocooned in my nice suburban home, even there, I know that Petros's church member was a sister of mine whose ugly death is a scandal that involves me too. I react as a Christian, but one who shares with Muslims a faith in God's dominion; with Hindus an understanding of the many faces of hope; with Buddhists, the Oneness throughout creation; with Jews, the shalom and work of healing God's broken handiwork.

Anglicans in the five southern African states estimate that over the next six years about 400,000 of their 4 million members will die of HIV/AIDS. Many, perhaps most, of those are mothers; many of those mothers' deaths will take with them the heart of the church's capacity to provide care for their own families and their communities.

What word do we have for one another? A word about the evil of HIV/AIDS is not enough, for that awful disease is only one subtle thread in the web that entangles us. Other sufferings bind us too: the burning of our planet; the violence of our thirty or forty "little" wars crackling at any given moment; the anger and hate that divide citizens from one another, nations from one another. The word that crawls across our TV and our imagination is terror. But no group of terrorists could possibly engender such a vast outpouring of fear that we rush to spend hundreds of billions of dollars to quell our anxieties and conquer our anxiousness. We react: alter centuries-old social contracts, shred the Constitution, rivet our attention on threats that lurk and shadows that disappear. Terrorists are probably amazed—and delighted—that our capacity to fear far exceeds their capacity to destroy. This book seeks to rebuild, to renew, our capacity to act out of hope rather than fear.

Mike Heisler, an old friend, and I frequently speculate what it would happen if all the assets of faith groups and health structures were to be aligned around a vision of a just and whole community. Mike, a medical doctor, abandoned his hands-off work as director of operations of the Task Force for Child Survival at the Carter Center for the nitty-gritty hands-on of public hospital medicine at Grady, Atlanta's downtown public hospital, where he serves occasionally as attending physician for the intensive care unit. This morning I go on rounds with him and his students, to see what happens when community fails. Surrounded by the high-tech world of modern medicine, I watch them pool brilliance, experience, intuition, and many hundreds of thousands of dollars of equipment into the effort to bring seven people back from the brink of death.

The patients were a complicated tangle of challenges, none of which involves guns or car wrecks. This is mundane disaster: advanced asthma (complicated by lifelong smoking);

pneumonia (vastly complicated by obesity); skyrocketing hypertension; a drug overdose that is really an unsuccessful suicide (marking despair over long-term cocaine addiction). One homeless 34-year-old guy has so many problems it was hard to know which is most likely to kill him first. None of these folks is insured, adding red ink to blood.

I am awed by the extravagant skill and attention lavished on people who have finally stumbled their way onto the edge of death. There they lie, amid the beeping machinery and furrowed brows, their every breath revealing a system of care that shows an astonishingly irrational respect for life, even the life of those least valued elsewhere. But back one step away from the precipice and the apparent sacredness of life declines rapidly. Care on what are called "step-down" wards is far less intimate and urgent. Care at the pharmacy is rationed severely. Care on the sidewalks seven floors down is damn near zero.

None of these people is really primarily a medical problem. Rather, their fragile health reflects a deep failure of many other systems. In those sterile-white hospital rooms, no charts report the pattern of bad choices, violent stress, isolation, and demeaning and alienating experiences of these patients, but anyone with a heartbeat could see them. Not all the bad choices were theirs personally, although some are obvious and spectacular. Failed or broken families, surely. Failed and broken schools and neighborhoods, probably. Failed and absent congregations—yes, certainly those too.

By the time these dedicated doctors and nurses get involved, all the rest of us have blown it. Teachers, coaches, pastors, friends, employers, county commissioners, school administrators, counselors, youth ministers, social service contactors, brothers, sisters, cousins, neighbors: all of us have failed to diagnose these end-stage problems when a cure was much more likely. When that web of responsibility and relationships fails, the body will find a way to die. When it is vital, we find a way to live.

Jimmy Carter once said, "We must make the choices that lead toward life." How does a community choose life? That is the question at the heart of this book.

A few years ago I was speaking at a conference in the San Francisco Bay area—always an adventure. The Reverend Cecil Williams was another of the speakers. Since his multithousand-member Glide Memorial Church was close by, he brought along his whole choir, which includes drums, electric guitars, and a startling (and colorful) array of professional singers, former prostitutes, and recently rehabilitated addicts. His choir is a wonder to behold, just sitting on stage. Its members do much more than sit. At one point in their mesmerizing performance, one of the women transfixed the audience with a song of survival and redemption called "Stand." That one word—powered by drums, guitars, a hundred voices—had the whole congregation standing on the pews joyfully waving our arms. This choir knew, and we began to see, the miracle of being able to stand after being crushed, broken, and despised.

But . . . what if we are not crushed, broken, and despised? What if we are only mildly depressed and distracted, worried about retirement or whether the second car needs a timing belt? Surely it is not enough just to stand there? The voice in my head says, "Hey, you—over on the side—quit standing there!" This book is for people who do not want to just stand around. More particularly, this is a book for those who may have the capacity to move with purpose and hope into the profound ambiguities of our modern communities, who are able to seek amid the brokenness and sickness a rebirth of wholeness and health.

If you are a person of faith who is sick of waiting for your institutions of faith to act faithfully, who cannot abide another week of standing around, this book is written for you. You may be paid to be faithful (the clergy), but I am not writing "how-tos" for the paid staff and professional side of faith. I seek to spend time with men and women who have something deep in their gut that feels like a scream trying to find voice, a tear trying to find an eye willing to weep, a muscle twitching eagerly for something heavy to lift.

You may work in thousands of places that do not bear the name of anything religious: public health offices, hospitals, jails, schools, day care centers. If you have hope that your life can align with the deepest hopes in your community, you are the one I want to talk with.

I am writing, of course, to and for myself too, lest I become accustomed—hardened—to the thousands of homeless on our streets, the smog-browned leaves of our forests, the millions dying of AIDS, the casual violence in and by our courts, the obscene neglect of our governments and our industries: the daily missed opportunities to bend ourselves toward hope and compassion. I write to remind myself and you, because I feel us edging toward surrender, in the honored way that the satisfied and complacent give up these days by claiming "the good life" as our privilege while the battles that matter rage just beyond our manicured lawns and mighty SUVs.

We need the same thing Petros needs: a word that will hold us true to whom we are, to what we have imagined, to our place, our task, our hope. And that word that matters has—is—a name.

In many cultures the giving of a name is a sacred defining act. In my culture it is rarely so. My wife and I named our daughters Lauren and Kathryn because we liked the sound of those names and thought our children should define themselves, rather than live out some relative or friend's history (which they have done). A name unfolds and finds meaning over time. A name reflects a personality and becomes a person. A name takes flesh and lives.

Navajos give their children "secret" names (Thinking Man, Woman Who Loves), names unknown and unused outside the intimate family but names that are simultaneously hopes for who the child will become and directions toward which she or he is to grow. The name is given not only to describe but also to inspire its bearer.

I want you to try on the name: boundary leader.

Discovering the Boundary Zone

The name "boundary leader" contains a way of seeing yourself. But it also contains a way of seeing your time and place and your webs of relationships.

Webster's Pocket Dictionary gives a simple definition of "boundary": "Anything forming or serving to indicate a limit or end."[1] Forget Webster. "Limits" and "ends" are the *not* how I am using the term.

Within the unlimited, endless boundaries of "boundary" leader, you will find that you know who you are, where you are, what you are to do there. You will find your own individual opportunities to build the capacity of others to choose life. You will find the zones, the places, where structures, ideals, organizations, visions, values—states of mind—bump against one another, those permeable walls where all our hopes, dreams, and aspirations can emerge.

A name may imply a task, a kind of work to do. The work of boundary leaders is to align the assets of community with the most relevant science and most mature faith. That seems impossibly naïve to people who have been numbed into passivity by containers of traditional management. For boundary leaders, that is the only reasonable standard of accountability they accept. Dr. Fred Smith, my teacher and friend, says that we have allowed ourselves to be out-organized by the forces of death, destruction, and disparity; and that it is time we organized ourselves in line with our aspirations for justice and healing. That means we have to begin by organizing ourselves guided by our principles, not theirs, to hold ourselves to appropriate standards.

As a boundary leader you will flip inside out and upside down, over and above, across and beyond the dominant boundary definitions of our time. The powers-that-be rest their confidence in organizations and networks, techniques for control and domination. Yet what goes on inside organizations and networks is peripheral, derivative, secondary, not of primary purpose or ultimate good. This is true whether the "organization" is the executive branch of the U.S. government or the "network" is a Lutheran association of pastors. The structures that pay us and often bind us are not the center; life orbits beyond their dominion. Boundary leaders know that structures, organizations, bureaucracies, and networks are temporary forms of allegiance with little if any permanent meaning. We are not created or defined by these organizational units. They are inadequate containers of our hopes. They deserve loyalty only to the extent they are part of the pattern of emergent life.

Our hopes and our fears dwarf our organizations and our networks just as surely as the wild cosmos mocked the fantastic pretensions of medieval powers. Like ancient myths of invincible gods and mighty kingdoms, our modern myths create illusions of omnipotent organizations and impregnable nations ruled through the transcendent power of wealth and force. Myths that confuse status quo with status approval, that place the way-things-are rather than the things-that-should-be at the center of the universe, are not neutral. They reinforce the sense of inevitability and thus passivity, just as surely as did the myth of personal impotence in medieval times. We mistake the temporary state for the more enduring reality, which is change. Because of the short time span of our experience, we vastly overrate the durability of the structures and forms that capture and control our lives, attitudes, outlooks, passions, and plans. We think our organizations are real stability, that instability is temporary. Thus we imagine that leadership is primarily about what happens inside organizations, inside structures.

Boundary leadership focuses on what is outside, beyond, across, between; on the opportunities that arise at the thin membrane of juncture; on the moments where one way, one vision, one idea, one value meets another way, vision, idea, value. Organizations exist and most of us most of the time are paid by them, spend time in them, care about them, use them—and often are abused by them. But a boundary leader's hopes lie beyond them, over, across, and beyond their boundaries. Anything that matters transcends all of our organizations or networks and so too must our leadership.

A boundary is exactly not where things separate, but the edge of where things join.

Boundary leadership thinks globally and locally, specifically applying its principles and plans to both immediate and distant need. It gives meaning and direction, whether the problem we face is the illness of an aging neighbor or AIDS in Africa, whether the pollution of a stream behind our house or global warming and the ecological destruction of our planet.

Boundaries are where things come together, where the fields of relationship engage. A boundary is exactly not where things separate, but the edge of where things join: physically, as between nations; legally, as between organizations; emotionally, as between values; mentally, as between ideas.

I have a piece of the Berlin wall on my desk. I picked it off the ground nearly forty years ago. Even in Berlin at the height of that fearful tyranny now dimly remembered as "communism," the field of relationship passed through the brick wall as easily as if it were smoke. My eighth-grade youth group could—and did—throw snowballs over it. Ideas did not even need to be thrown; they passed through at the speed of radio waves and light, as the brightness of West Berlin domed both halves of the divided city. Walls and brick and wire, machine guns and tank traps, turned out to be weak, porous, and now long gone.

Many of the stories to follow describe boundaries that seem stable and firm but are permeable, less substantial than they appear. Like the Berlin wall, the fact that lines and walls are porous gives home to those who fear them and fear to those who trust them. Boundary leaders appreciate that the world is filled with many kinds of dividing lines, but look to the greater realities that span them and find that they have fewer fears and more hopes.

Political boundaries look stable and important on our maps. Here is Alabama; here is Georgia. If you are a Georgian, or if you are an Alabamian, it matters which is which and where the line is. Atlanta is busily sprawling with little attention to old lines. If you could lay a century or two of maps on top of one another, you would quickly see that the lines move back and forth, constantly negotiated, sometimes fought over. Empires big and little want us to take their maps seriously: ours, theirs, mine. They want us to treat minor distinctions as if they were significant.

Boundary leaders look at the zone over which the boundaries have moved and are moving so they can operate at the scale of the whole phenomenon, the entire system. Boundary leaders do not confine their intelligence inside temporary insignificant containers that will change and shift before truly significant phenomena. Atlanta's capacity to sprawl thoughtlessly across the pine forests will be stopped by a real boundary—the limited watershed—not some meaningless line on the ground. Boundary leaders think and lead at the level of the whole system. So we keep asking about what the system is that matters: the system of AIDS, violence, sprawl, and despair.

Counselors and psychotherapists encourage people to protect their boundaries in order to secure their identity; good advice for those who have been damaged and wounded. But even—especially—among humans, boundaries are seldom clear and clean. We are our relationships. In Africa it is said: "I am because we are." The "me" inside my boundaries is pretty small and not likely to survive apart from the entirety of us. We

are whom we engage. The very notion of distinct separation is
an illusion. The world that surrounds us is also inside us.

When you move beyond the boundaries, you may notice
that you do not immediately move into another defined space.
Indeed, in most communities there is a space between clear
definitions that I call the boundary zone.

Boundary zones, those areas where boundaries are least
stable and most in flux, are where most things that matter happen. People who are most vitally alive cannot stay away.
Population, global warming, HIV/AIDS, environmental
issues, human rights, early childhood problems—all draw us
beyond our narrow disciplines and organizations toward
boundary zones. The space is attractive not only because of
ghoulish interest in suffering, but because those zones of pain
are also zones of vital response. We want to be where our lives
matter the most, where our muscles, brains, and spirits are
stretched to their intended purposes.

We learn from nature that life is born where water and
land come together. Georgia holds one of the great vital
boundary zones in North America, the vast lowland marshes
of Glynn. Here the tides are often seven to nine feet, extend-
ing wetland marshes miles inland. This verdant muck cradles
a significant fraction of sea and bird life.

Where does earth end and sea begin? The question
obscures the answer: the "boundary" moves in a tide of constant change that is the engine of life. If we draw our lines here
or there, we risk destroying the whole system. Our urge to
contain, mark, and constrain is deadly to this interwoven system, of which we are part. At various times in the past the
whole network of islands, marshes, and rivers has moved miles
from where it happens to be now. It will move again. It is moving, just like our human communities move. Knowing that is
far more important than knowing where an artificial line is
drawn this moment.

Boundary leadership ignores the lines and moves over,
into, beyond, across, among vital emergent zones. It gives

priority to the expansive, endless, and open against the insular, interior, parochial, and delimited. Boundary leaders may function in and amid structures and organizations, but they never confuse them as ultimate or even lasting. Boundary leaders focus on what endures and what matters: relationships and the values and commitments that shape and sustain relationships.

The name "boundary leader" describes not only who we are, but also where we are, and what we could be doing here. It makes it possible not only to have integrity in the sense of making our actions consistent with our identity, but also to be integral, to make our identity consistent with and part of a larger reality. Growing into that name makes it possible for us to act with deep purpose and moral conviction. This has practical effects for the organizations we work for and through and around, the neighborhoods we live in, the children we love. If we are wrong about the implications of this name, the results of our life will be accidental at best. If we are right, we find ourselves aligned with all that matters. We experience the most profound gift a human can experience—the sense that one's slender strengths and handful of years are part of the emergence of God's intentions for the world.

A boundary leader hopes for the whole system, not just his or her own sphere. This focus on whole systems is what distinguishes boundary leaders from old-fashioned managers, but it also is what distinguishes grown-ups from children. Boundary leadership is a move toward maturity, away from adolescent obsession with myself and my stuff. A child may display compassion; a lone adult may show fairness. A boundary leader pushes beyond personal virtues and values toward whole systems that care, systems that move toward life. A boundary leader does so in the highly ambiguous and contested spaces of the boundary zones. The boundary zones call out and make relevant the full menu of assets, the rich interpersonal store of powers that bear on the future. As Fred Smith noted, we have been out-organized by the forces of despair, which *do* function at the level of whole cultures and ecosystems while we chip away at endless lists of symptoms. Boundary leaders think at the scale of the whole so their efforts are organized properly.

Most of what matters on earth happens at the boundaries: scientific breakthroughs, toppling of apartheid, institution of universal health care, equity for all human beings. Most of the leadership that matters happens there too. The boundary separating church and state, supposedly marked by an impregnable wall, is in constant friction and negotiation or engagement. So too the boundary between ideas and ideologies, between two nations, between rich and poor, white and people of color. The closer we look, the less we find distinctions, separation, isolation.

Boundary zones delineate this area of ambiguity and opportunity. The heart of my hope lies there, at the boundary zone, and there, in the life of the boundary leader.

Becoming Together

Dr. William Foege, visionary global health leader, once noted, "You don't need to know where you are to be there. But if you want to go somewhere else, it is the first thing you need to know." Likewise, you do not need to know who you are to be who you are. Most have given up hope on the possibilities of living lives of meaning and purpose. So we slide from birth to death wearing others' swirls, stripes, and logos, never living up to our own name for ten minutes of our lives. The simple purpose of this book is to remind you of a name, an identity, a way to see your life and work that is truly yours to live. A right name invites you deeply into your center. It invites you to tread the ground on which you walk as your own true path.

Your name of "boundary leader" does not come without tension. For a boundary leader works with a shoulder to the boundary itself; one pushes, pulls, shoves, nudges, nurses,

institutes, and develops the shifts and movement that create
new boundaries. Knowing yourself as a boundary leader may
draw you away from the paths others would have you walk, but
at the same time toward the paths that lead in directions you
believe in and cherish. One friend, hearing the boundary
leader identity for the first time, confessed that he recognized
himself but did not like it. "This is not what I was raised for.
No wonder I'm off on the edge of my organization and my
profession!" Another expressed the same feelings when first I
named her a boundary leader. "But," she confessed, "this is who
I am; it is the way I live, it is the way I work, it is where my
power and vitality live."

The practical implications to knowing your name dictate
the structure of this book. In the next chapter we will examine
the nature of boundary zones through the lens of disparities in
health, and we will explore possible pathways for transforming
our communities to eliminate those disparities. We will spend
time looking at the inside and outside patterns of boundary
leadership (although both come to a complete halt if separated
for any longer than a paragraph or two). Then we will look at
the webs of transformation in which boundary leadership
develops, works, and is sustained. Finally, I will suggest a way
of life, a pattern of faith—and struggle with faith—that is typical of boundary leadership.

Now may be the time to say what this book is not. Because I am
interested in community-scale issues, the book may appear to
offer lessons on how to run your organization, for politics or
social change, for theology, and/or for a career path. Boundary
leadership engages all of those, but in the process pushes them
from the center to the periphery, which is where they make sense.

So:

• This book will not be particularly helpful in teaching you
  how to run an organization better. I have little to add to the

zillion books that claim to teach one how to run an organization. I do engage some key organizational thinkers, dragging them out into the boundary zone. For instance, the work of Terrence Deal in *Reframing Organizations* is profoundly helpful in understanding boundary zones, even though it was not intended to do that. Boundary leadership is not oblivious to structures, but reorganizes organizational thinking. Indeed, it places the whole art of management into its proper context: interior management becomes a subset of whole-system engagement. Boundary leaders do run things; they just never mistake that as the heart of what matters.

- This book offers no political scheme to impose one's great ideas on the rest of the neighborhood, much less city, much less nation or world. Other books and consultants eagerly (though rarely effectively) teach you how to subdue others to your will. Old-fashioned manipulative politics greatly magnified by tools of communication are quite likely to be the death of us and all forms of life on the planet, so I do not want to add any more schemes to the bonfire. Boundary leadership embodies a strategy for change at the level of the whole system, but it is exactly *not* the cynical politics of division, distraction, and destruction. Boundary leadership is smart enough about power to help you avoid being sucked into its ancient whirlpool. What makes boundary leadership spiritual is precisely its understanding of the depth of that ancient trap. The existence of an alternative will not help you manipulate others. But you may find yourself less anxious about other people's plans.

- This book is not going to help you fine-tune your systematic theology or any other "-ology." I take theological discourse very seriously and wish for more and deeper discourse. Boundary leadership multiplies the complexity and challenge of practicing the principles of clearly enunciated theology, however, because it lives in a gray area of shifting lines, where neither control nor clarity is promised. It is rare to find a theological discussion anywhere nearly as edifying as the lived-out sophistication and faithfulness experienced quite commonly in the webs of relationships of boundary leaders. You just cannot be in the webs of boundary leadership and avoid asking the deep questions that drive you like a stiff wind in heavy seas. While it is hard to keep a systematic theology together, you will trust in your sails and in God's grace more.

- This book probably will not help your career. Indeed, it may endanger the career you are in as you rethink your path. The upside is that you might like your life a lot more—gone will be the dissonance, the jangling sense of a life at odds with your values and your interests—once you get accustomed to, grow into, your true name. Boundary leaders have unpredictable careers but rewarding lives. I recommend that you keep the book away from your boss. If, however, your organization is even partly dependent on successfully engaging complex community dynamics, you might find a way to slip a copy onto the boss's desk (anonymously, of course). If you have anyone working for you, you need them to understand boundary leadership so they can figure out what the heck you are doing with your life (and theirs!).

- The book does not have much data or evidence in it—odd considering I am on the faculty at a School of Public Health where we *really* like to count things. The notion of boundary leadership is driven by an intense commitment to base our lives and our commitments on things as they actually are. This is frequently more integrated and whole than the categories in which we count and sort things. So while I do not offer the numbers, you may find here an argument for a much more intensive respect for the whole phenomenon our data describe.

- Finally, this book will not make you a boundary leader. It is the last thing from a bag of tricks. It may, however, reveal the boundary leader potential simmering within. I once thought that boundary leaders were a tiny minority working on remote (if vital) fringes. I now see that the boundary zones

constitute most of what matters and that nearly all of us
sense a call across the false divides. We are born for the
whole, not the part; born to be integral, not partial.
Becoming who you are is less like performing others' tricks
(even mine) and more like waking up.

The call to boundary leadership is already within you.
You may already be a great plumber, public health leader,
lawyer, school teacher, businesswoman, doctor, carpenter,
house-husband—whatever. I suspect you hope for more. The
promise of boundary leadership should feel like a call from
home asking for help.

And maybe even more. For until you sense the boundary leader you are, you will feel discordant due to the tension
between your deepest call and the partial identity that contains you. The more you succeed at the partial, the less it will
satisfy your deepest sense of the whole. It is in that "practice"
of boundary leadership that your life, though perhaps not
always harmonious, will find harmony with the divine image
you are intended to mature.

A year or so ago I had lunch with Bill Bolling and an
incredibly sincere student about to graduate from Brown
University. Over the past two decades, Bill has been a poster
person for boundary leadership in Atlanta, beginning as a
community minister at St. Luke's Episcopal Church, where he
started one of the first (if not the first) food banks in the
United States. The Metro Food Bank now provides industrial-
scale support to more than seven hundred nonprofit organizations in the city. Bill is an essential part of nearly every high
level discussion at which boundary zone issues are engaged
here, from homelessness to regional leadership to interfaith
collaboration. Bill and I live about three blocks from each
other and from time to time have breakfast together in a local
café or talk while our daughters play high school soccer.

On this occasion, I was to help the graduate student
choose her next steps, which she more or less described as a

choice between helping some disastrously poor African village and helping some similarly distressed U.S. slum. I suggested this was a lousy way to choose a life, wondering how it would feel to be the chief of the African village upon finding that he lived in the absolutely worst dump in the entire world. Instead I told her to follow her sense of where life was trying to break out, to find people whom she just had to be around because they made her feel more alive and vital. In my experience, Africa competes pretty well in that category, but maybe not for her. When you move toward life, you move toward others moving toward life and find yourself among a web of lively and interesting people.

Boundary leadership is a subject without clear boundaries. It is a bit like politics or ethics because leadership is about everything that matters. It is about what we humans do on purpose about our fears and our hopes. How that happens in any particular group depends on many things, one of which is the character, discernment, and competence of the group's leaders. We begin by being accountable for who we are, for what influence we have on our relationships that connect us to others.

At its most basic level, leadership is saying yes to what matters most—giving meaning and value to the incremental steps that are the next right things to do. The critical leadership act is to lend weight to the appropriate measures, values, and standards that illuminate the pathway toward what matters most. It is not so much about getting others to do this act or to behave that way. Rather, it is first about living lives of integrity that are aligned with the choices that lead toward life. The skill sets, the competencies, the strategies are footnotes. In that sense, much of this book is a long footnote, for we will shine the light of boundary leadership through those facets: kaleidoscopic patterns of relationships among leaders, the internal work of formation and then external transformation, the way of living and even the prisms of spiritual growth.

Scott Russell Sanders describes his impatience with writers who type their way into false comfort:

It is as though we have built a great bonfire,
and we are heaping onto it everything we can seize—
hawks and herrings, swamps and mountains, rivers and soil.
If I open a book written in our time, and I do not hear the
crackle of flames,
I soon close it again, not because I enjoy the reminder of havoc,
but because I cannot take seriously an art that ignores this
holocaust.
We are quick to condemn our ancestors who ignored slavery
or apartheid or pogroms or the abuse of women and children.
Those who follow us, and inherit from us a severely damaged
world,
will surely look back on our time
and ask what we were doing while the earth burned.[2]

I cannot bear to contribute one more fallacious hope to the stack of modern fantasies. I do not suggest that any mere leadership model is adequate for the interweave of planetary crises we face. I can say that leaders drawn to those issues that matter most tend to move toward and then push against boundaries because there they find not just hope but also remedies. As they do so, they create webs of transformation in which their own hope and own responses resonate with the hopes and responses of others, and they create in that resonance patterns of new relationships that transform the structures and powers that otherwise trap us short of hope. In those new relationships, we find ways of realigning the structures and assets in our communities and at larger scales.

> Our boundary leaders know very well the reality of what "is," but allow themselves to be accountable to what "could be."

Much of this book is about another grief, the pervasive and enduring disparity between races. I cannot take seriously a book that does not ache there, for such inequity is the obvious link between the rain of death of AIDS in Africa and the durable shame of own national complacency. Leadership that is not intentional about the durable brokenness among our one human race is a distraction and indulgence, confined to managing the fires in the back lot of the empire.

But I am writing to clarify our hope, not our fear. This book describes the hopeful way of leading that I see emerging in the heart of the most difficult communities, the most profound sorrow, the most persistent problems.

The poet William Stafford recalls that his son, Kim, was reading Stafford's poems for an audience when a voice blurted from out of the darkness: "I could have written that."

"But you didn't," said Stafford, looking down at the upturned face.

He waited one beat of silence. "But you could write your own."

Throughout this book, I present brief vignettes of boundary leaders who are "writing their own," whose lives are becoming the words we seek to express not only to describe the task of assaulting the boundaries that divide, confine, separate, isolate, and insulate, but also to illumine the hope, promise, opportunity, love, and compassion that instills and nurtures and motivates such commitment.

Born of a perception, our boundary leaders know very well the reality of what "is," but allow themselves to be accountable to what "could be." Each is responding to the yawning gap between those two in his or her own way and thus becoming, in life, the words we are listening for. Each is part of a healing web of transformation.

Our examples are pastors and theologians; some work in community-based organizations, some are doctors or nurses. They do not offer a list of tips and to-dos. None would say, "Do it this way." Rather they offer us an invitation: "Come this way—into the boundary zones." And we find that we want to do so and that it is possible.

If you care about the whole world in its completeness, then the invitation to the boundary zones is one hard to resist.

Where else do you go? We, you and I, are among a growing web of people drawn toward the possibilities of transformation and, in doing so, toward one another. We are finding life, and faith, in the shifting zones where boundaries meet—abundant, vital, rich, emergent. It is a kind of life, a kind of faith, as vital and as practical as the soil from which all things draw life and to which all things return.

It is no small thing to recognize that thousands of boundary leaders are at work creating the webs of transformation that make hope possible. Many of us may recognize in boundary leadership a model that describes what we have already been doing (even when we thought we were doing something else). You may sense relief at finally knowing who you are. I do not want you to stop at that point, but rather to push toward excellence. Boundary leadership, like old-fashioned management, can be done well or carelessly. The world needs your very best and I hope to help you do just that.

Who can say if our lives will be enough and in time? But then, who can say that they won't? So, come this way.

2

Boundary Zones

Say the word "boundary" and you tend to think of lines: a fence line, a state or national border, the Berlin wall, or the new Israeli wall. If a boundary is a line, it would seem to preclude any space between. Where one boundary ends, another starts. It is the edge of things. This approach gives itself to delineations of "thrones and dominations," as Dorothy Sayers noted. In this world, change can mean moving the boundary (as Saddam Hussein tried to do when he declared Kuwait part of Iraq) or adopting a new title that fits the glorious nature of the bounded domain (I think half the Baptist "pastors" in Atlanta have exalted themselves as being bishops). The harder the lines, the tighter the identities.

Boundary leaders see through and beyond the lines of demarcation, keeping their eyes on the fluid zones between them and around them. Boundary leaders think of their community as a kind of estuary in which salt water and fresh water mingle. Salt water has life. Fresh water has life. But if you really want to see what life in and of the water can be, go to Chesapeake Bay where they mingle. Estuaries and their counterpart, wetlands, these "edge" environments, are incredibly rich, attracting all those who love complex environments. It demands a type of leader adapted to thrive in its particular ecology. Estuary communities attract boundary leaders.

As we move into the nature of boundary zone, it might be easier to clarify what is not boundary zone terrain. When I started noticing boundary leaders I thought they were a tiny band on the edge (of course) and that their zone was narrow. It is the reverse, but there is still a crucial place for bounded organizations where boundary leadership does not help. Old styles and techniques of management are going to be with us for some time, and where they are helpful, we should be grateful. Within certain organizational enclaves old-fashioned management is viable, although the number of such circumstances is shrinking every day. Places where boundary leadership is *not* necessary include those where:

1. The tasks to be accomplished are clear and stable and the credentials relevant to the tasks are also clear to everyone involved (including supervisor, supervised, clients, and stakeholders).
2. The standards of performance and accomplishment are agreed on (what exactly are "good job" and "bad job"), and those standards remain stable when personnel change.
3. There is a dependable and adequate flow of resources that value the process in a predictable way.
4. There is a stable market for the process that values the process in a predictable way.
5. There is adequate control of all factors including people, intellectual property, and the old-fashioned factors of production. A major part of "control" derives from the clear agreement on objective standards that define "appropriate" relationships among these factors. Thus "control" means largely ensuring adherence to existing standards, not forcing new partners into new roles.
6. There are strong, clear internal lines of accountability that everyone understands that do not need to be continually defined or negotiated.

7. There are simple, appropriate, objective, external accountability standards (Did the stock go up? Do we have more
   money than we started with? Do we have more members?).
   These standards are valued as legitimate by key stakeholders and partners.

There may be some situations that fulfill those criteria, but
not many. For instance, management of nuclear waste process-
ing facilities would seem to demand management in line with
all seven. The stuff has a dangerous half-life of thousands of
years during which time it must not be allowed into the
ecosystem. Even those that seem to fit are still buffeted by
larger boundary phenomena (one thinks of the constantly
rolling scientific debate about adequate standards for ensuring
the waste does not damage groundwater and who is qualified
to comment).

In large enterprises or complex organizations, some
facets of the overall process allow themselves to be governed
under the old leadership. But a close look at what seem from
the outside to be simple, predictable enterprises shows that
they actually fulfill few of the criteria for old-fashioned,
command-and-control leadership. Some aspects of banking
might have allowed for old-style management, but no longer.
Wherever old-management thinking is visible in banking,
one can almost paint the bull's-eye on the side of the building, for someone is guaranteed to be planning to take over or
outsource that process.

It is not uncommon for boundary leaders to be paid by
organizations that are still operating on old models of performance. Indeed, many boundary leaders do boundary work
incognito or apologize the whole time for not being good
internal managers. We live in both worlds, managing a
process by old standards (which may be appropriate), such as
an immunization program or soup kitchen, while we try to do
the work outside the walls, aligning structures as best we can
with stolen time.

Leadership is appropriate depending on whether it is suited to its social ecology. Come with me into this rich ecological zone of the boundaries.

Boundary Zoning

Some lines matter more than others. Politicians know that the boundary between the United States and Mexico is clearly defined and legally fixed. But that only matters to the extent that the bounded identity fits reality. Birds and butterflies fail to respect the border, following instead the lines of natural systems that have made their lives possible since long before two-legged mammals started drawing maps at all.

Ask any Hispanic maid living in a Los Angeles barrio, any Hispanic carpenter working on a West Dallas construction site, any Hispanic child of a migrant laborer harvesting wheat from a Kansas field—ask any of these, and millions more, about the boundary between the United States and Mexico, and they will describe a more flexible, fluid, and complex relationship than the one described by the politicians and cartographers. The political border is only one way to describe the relationship between the phenomenon of Mexico and the phenomenon of the next nation to the north. Taking the political line too seriously obscures the complexity of the relationship.

Somewhere south of the Rio Grande and north of the next job opportunity, next family connection, next crop to pick, lies the Mexican-American boundary zone. It is a thousand-mile moving zone in which the relationship is intensive, constantly negotiated, felt, fought, and feared. Many aspects of the relationship operate within this zone of engagement. If you live there, it is helpful to expect complexity no matter what role you play. You might simply be a Methodist Church member in Kansas noticing a stream of Spanish-speaking people in the emergency rooms. You might be a county health officer trying to figure out what do with uninsured Spanish-speaking kids in schools. You might be the one English speaker in your family with a sick brother, having to take the day off from school to go with your mom to translate in the ER. The point is, you need a mental model of your life that fits the complexity of what is real. The boundary zone is not a line anywhere, but a zone that stretches hundreds of miles. That may be daunting, but reality is daunting, too.

This way of turning on the lights to the complexity of the boundary zones also fits the spaces among organizations, networks, businesses, churches, and communities. Indeed, all human bordered entities, mental or physical, are more like boundary zones than clearly contained things. As long as we think this zone is a merely temporary phenomenon, we will miss the fundamental nature of our world: the loss of perimeter, the porous nature of every identity.

Any unit that has "boundaries" by any name—organizations, businesses, networks, tribes, nation/states—whatever humans can conceive to have distinguishable limitations, can be more accurately seen to be flexible, borderless, in motion like waves, as unstable as sand before sea, as predictable as sunrise and sunset. We say, "as different as night and day," and forget dusk and the movement of endless variety of night skies and colors before dawn. Even a bird-sized brain knows that the light in the forest is different with every glance.

Boundary zones are places of conflict in which the powerful always try to protect what they have from what they fear. Perhaps no greater evidence of physical boundary zones exists than in the dozens of wars that flame this moment across our globe: thousands die for the sake of disputed lines drawn shakily on old maps. My tribe does not recognize the validity of your tribe's border: we kill each other, and our war thrives in the broken spaces contested by both of us, outside the control of either of us.

Boundary zones are not empty; they are fields of relationship and power. In battles as bloody as a Bosnian village, as devastating as decisions made in an Enron boardroom, we die for and within boundary zones.

Boundary zones are shaped by innumerable factors: highly complex, large-scale shifts, they blow outside our old ways of describing the conditions and circumstances in which we find our "universe" and ourselves. Within the Mexico–United States boundary zone, we find order and control that is contested, for it is a place and a phenomenon of numerous interacting forces that include, but are not confined to, technology, ecological destruction, overpopulation, political expediency—where need and greed engage.

The idea that lines of identity and control are transient and porous is deeply disturbing to those of us raised to expect a world of organization and power. The whole globe looks fearful to those accustomed to being shielded by traditional political tools of wealth, violence, and coercion. As a white middle-class American, that applies to me. Is there anything stronger than those tools in which I can trust? No wonder the Chinese built a Great Wall and the Americans fenced south Arizona; no wonder the East Germans built the Berlin wall and the Israelis are building a wall to keep out the Palestinians: if the lines are working for us, we like to think them permanent, part of the universe's trajectory. Those whose aspirations for life are denied may feel quite differently and hope for a liberating God who subverts and destabilizes the powerful in favor of justice—sort of like the God of the ancient prophets.

> The challenge of boundary leadership is to live in the world as it is, refusing the illusionary security of lines that do not in fact divide, the deceptive simplicity that masks the underlying complexity.

We may feel differently about boundary zones depending on where we are raised and how we benefit from them. But whatever our feelings, they simply are. The challenge of boundary leadership is to live in the world as it is, refusing the illusionary security of lines that do not in fact divide, the deceptive simplicity that masks the underlying complexity.

Natural and human interconnectedness, by crossing (ignoring) boundaries, creates boundary zones that, over time and with energy, are seldom if ever clear, stable, or certain. Physicists use the term "chaos" to describe systems without apparent order. Boundary zones appear to have no order, but they just have a more complex order than our simplified identity admits. When we submit to the complexity that actually is, we are drawn into newly ordered relationships that are appropriate. The nature of the chaotic system creates the forms of relationship that thrive in it: simple identities for simple contained systems; complex identities for boundary zones. Although I have a simple identity as a middle-class white guy, when forced, I realize I have a much more layered identity built on many relationships that are not always visible or conscious. I am a father of daughters, a member of an ancient, highly diverse religious tradition, linked by friendship with many in Africa and Europe (and even a handful of Asians). I am a fiftyish mammal who still plays basketball, a carnivore with a dog named Henry, owner of a cabin on what used to be—and perhaps what should still be—Cherokee land. All of these define me more accurately than my simple identity. In the complexity, I am able to see that I am already drawn past my simple lines into the real world.

But Why? So What?

Two questions mark the way into the boundary zone: But why? So what? The first is the magnet that pulls us into the boundary zone; the second is the mold that shapes the work of the boundary leader. If we do not ask the first, it is highly unlikely that our answer to the second will make any sense.

A serious "But why?" almost always leads across organizational boundaries. It also usually leads outside any one discipline or field of expertise or experience. In the process it leads into a broad, often-confusing and -invigorating range of odd relationships. This creates predictable patterns of perceived strengths and weaknesses. A serious "So what?" leads in the same way to commitment, committees, and coalitions as your path becomes entangled with others who are asking similar questions. This creates a pattern of skills and competencies of those who become boundary leaders.

It would be so much simpler if we could keep all the issues in some rational containers in which they could be engaged in sequence and priority. We would not need boundary leadership if we could stay inside our familiar urn. The problem is that almost nothing that matters fits or stays in such containers. Anything that matters leads us toward the boundary zone. Until you understand that, you will tend to think that the real adult work happens inside the containers of our institutions. We find security in this notion, for it protects us from the wild and deep seas that surge in the boundary zones. But we might trust a different security if we thought there was a kind of leadership adequate to its challenge. I think there is.

Many theologies see that all brokenness is connected, just as is all healing. So I am not arguing that racial disparities are a higher priority than ecological catastrophes, religious violence, population growth, or global warming. But for an American, there is no greater test of our most basic fears and hopes than the intractable patterns of racial disparities, which turn out to hold steady decade after decade across a wide range of indicators of well-being. Both persistence and range mock our desire to manage our way out of the situation. Billions of dollars of programs aimed at one separate problem after another leave the basic gap astonishingly untouched. Does it help to look at race as a boundary zone kind of issue? Come with me into this deep water and see for yourself.

Understanding Sadie

Sadie worked for my family when I was growing up in Baltimore; she was the first black person I can remember knowing. While still young—in her sixties—Sadie died of what we understand to be complications of diabetes, about twenty years earlier than my mother died. Nothing could be less surprising to anyone familiar with life in these United States. As an African American woman, Sadie was statistically much more likely to suffer diabetes than my mother. But why?

The difference in life span between Sadie and my mother is more dramatic than the statistical white-black average, which is *only* about seven years. But it was about the same difference in longevity and quality of life experienced by their mothers. There is a good chance that a similar difference in span of life and health will occur between Sadie's *granddaughter* and my *daughters*. Although each generation of black women and white women for the past one hundred years has experienced a significant average increase in life span, the difference between those of the same age has remained astonishingly stable.[1] Over that century, there have been extraordinary changes in medicine, public health, access to voting, employment, law, communications, transportation, patterns of employment, and housing. Yet even as averages improve for everyone, the gap remains between black and white. But why?

If, in seeking our answer, we question Sadie's personal behaviors and health habits, we will not get far in understanding what is happening to generations of Sadies—nor will we have a clue how to break the pattern. "What did Sadie do to cause her problem?" is exactly the wrong question. Jonathan Lomas, writing in *Social Science and Medicine*, explores how the discipline of public health has largely focused on individual-level behaviors and interventions, instead of exploring environmental factors and social processes.[2] Rather than examine the contribution of social, economic, and racial patterns to community health (and therefore individually to Sadie's health), he argues, complacent and complicit epidemiologists have focused myopically on Sadie's conduct and family history. The result: a precise answer to the wrong question. Nothing makes us dumber quicker than that.

The disciplines that currently dominate the health policy world—economics and biomedical science—have deep within them a core assumption that the individual is an appropriate unit of measurement, analysis, and modification. They accept the individual boundaries as real. Individual behaviors and choices are the causes that explain what happens, what really matters. Reality is more or less a huge accumulation of individual decisions, all made within boundaries between the individuals. Any unit of measurement above the individual person is considered to be just a statistical construct: interesting, but not real. I exaggerate, but not by much. The cause-effect models that flow from these individualistic assumptions do not credit the existence of something called "the public." The community is "a heap of individuals" rather than a system, a unity to be engaged, altered, and held accountable. When they read, "Hear, O Israel, I am your God," they are stumped: there is no Israel with a God, just a gaggle of Israelites, each of whom individually has one of its own gods. Today we can hardly imagine a Yahweh holding the United States accountable for the sin of complacency in the deadly disparities that mock justice.

Sadie's face helps me look to her sisters, family, and neighborhood in a way that ultimately reflects my own face in the mirror. Sadie died from diabetes, as best we knew at the time. This is only one disease in which disparities between white and black Americans are visible and persistent. What makes diabetes a boundary zone issue is that the pattern of disparities is found in multiple diseases and causes of early death. Policy makers trying to engage the problem speak of a "big six" agenda of disparities: cardiovascular disease, diabetes, cancers, HIV/AIDS, immunization, and infant mortality. The most obvious thing about all six is that they are deeply interwoven. They are also all linked by more fundamental factors than the diseases themselves. Although health specialists tend to lead the discussion, the causes—determinants—of the disease categories lie far beyond mere medical language, and thus far beyond the qualifications of physicians and medical researchers to map. The data draw us deep into shame and mystery; indeed, the more clear the numbers, the more shameful and mysterious they are.

African Americans represent about one-eighth of the U.S. population, but more than one-third (37 percent) of the 700,000 AIDS cases. Nearly half of all African American deaths in 1999 were from AIDS—they are not only far more likely to have the disease, but also more likely to die quickly from it. The death rate of blacks from AIDS exceeds same-age whites by a staggering 655 percent. In 1999 the incidence for new HIV cases among black women was 50 for every 100,000; it was 3 for every 100,000 white women.[3] Understanding the medical character of the virus will get you only to the door of this mystery. AIDS pulls us into the boundary zone in which generational patterns of race, gender relationships, oppression, and economics ripple and twist in ways that humble any one of our specialty disciplines.

It is not remotely enough simply to put our little solutions next to one another so that one of us contributes caregiving, another gives access to medicine, another develops prevention education messages, another works on a vaccine, another deals with stigma. No, the answer to the disparity in death rates among black Americans and white Americans is more complex, more devious, more difficult: it is to be found only within the boundary zone, where we are driven to stop dealing with discrete symptoms and start examining linked causes. It is unethical not to do so when the disparities are so stunning.

Most committees stagger at the prospect of entering that boundary zone; they find it safer and easier to continue figuring out how to open enough hospital beds, how to move the mobile van around, how to get speakers and brochures in all the churches. Committee members are pleased to find a concrete task that can ameliorate at least one aspect of the suffering. But their premature relief is defeated as soon as they walk out on the street and look around at the untouched tangle that mocks their incremental gain.

Cancer offers another disturbing window into disparities. There are many kinds of cancer, multiple apparent causes. Yet disparities are remarkably consistent. Given: genetic tendencies may account for some differences in particular types of cancer. Given: genetic differences may create predispositions for similar types of cancers. But the dramatic and stable gap between the occurrence of cancer among whites and that among blacks—crossing so many types of cancers with such strikingly different patterns of causes—forces us to deeper factors and thus into the boundary zone. The specific conceptual containers have little power to explain what is happening and thus what to do. But why?

A couple of years ago I was meeting in an executive suite with the senior staff of a powerful hospital owned by Wake Forest University. The sun filtered through a penthouse skylight, bounced off polished wood before disappearing into a thick dark carpet that muted our conversation. Daily this group of leaders makes decisions about hundreds of jobs and millions of dollars—not to mention the many *humans* living and dying in their building.

We were sitting atop a medical castle that dominates the skyline of Winston-Salem, which at the time had the highest infant mortality rate in the state of North Carolina. This fact was not only an intellectual curiosity and ethical quandary, but also a political sand trap. At some point the citizens of the state were bound to question why this place of privilege had so little relevance to the most obvious priority: the survival of its youngest children born into highly conflicted boundary zones. Even though the hospital had recently purchased a clinic in the middle of the most affected neighborhood, it found it difficult to cross the boundaries into the lives of the children. These good and powerful men felt no more authority than one of their janitors, what with insurance companies, doctors' guilds, unions, lawyers, and bondholders. Indeed, almost none of the adults in the city considered themselves free, much less obliged, to fulfill the most primal function of every grown mammal—to protect its young. So the children of Winston-Salem die.

Infant mortality is a highly complex phenomenon. Surely, one thinks, only so many things could go wrong so quickly in life! Yet consider the disparities of national statistics: of every 1,000 children less than one year old, 7 die; the average for white children, however, is below that: 5.5 kids per 1,000; while the African American rate is is closing in on being three times higher than the white rate.[4]

For the "disease" of infant mortality, there is no pill available, no drive-by solution. One must see the moving boundaries of poverty, race, nutrition, housing, too-young mothers and their despair. In Winston-Salem the highest rates of infant mortality are concentrated in African American neighborhoods. Race is not just one boundary, however, but a nested set of interlocking factors.[5] Race is linked to but different from poverty. Penetrating slightly deeper in the "But why?" might lead one toward the fact of low-pay service-industry jobs and pervasive lack of health insurance, which precludes access to skilled medical services except in crisis. One would need to understand the profound implications of multigenerational poverty, low self-esteem, and reduced expectations in the context of highly promoted consumer models of success.[6] The pervasive scent of tobacco offers up another clue about power and pathology.

How would one begin to align the complex community assets around such an obvious and deeply linked scandal? I will not be giving away the end of the book to suggest that boundary leaders do just that with no need for simplistic illusions of quick answers.

Disparities' Disparity:
Race as Boundary Zone

Any problem significant enough to make it into the newspapers turns out to be nearly as complex as infant mortality: crime, teen pregnancy, random violence, AIDS, urban sprawl, environmental decay, immigration, even the decline of songbirds. Health pathologies are multifactorial, historical, tangled, and contested because they are social and systemic. Pathologies tend to be understood in terms of their past, as if the determinants are behind us, only coming to the surface now. Actually, it is more helpful to see each of the components as part of a stream of factors whose influence contributes and conflicts over time in a complex interplay even affecting how and if the pathology is perceived at all. ("Premature" infant mortality itself reflects social expectations that move and change.)

Why all these disparities based on race? Why do they persist across generations when so much else changes?

A major advance in understanding what is at play here—the social dynamics of disparities—has been emerging in the boundary zone in between many disciplines drawn to the intractable nature of race and racism amid wealth (see figure 1). Discrimination (whether it applies to racial or ethnic minorities, women, homosexuals, or groups of different ages) is a stressful phenomenon that can influence disease processes through a number of potential pathways. Discrimination—especially when it is internalized—is a kind of contagion that affects the functioning of physical organs just like "real" diseases. It *is* real.[7]

This linking of race to health is multidimensional. It considers biological factors, cultural factors, socioeconomic factors, political factors, and racism itself, all of whose effects flow through a variety of pathways to affect health outcomes.

At this point we step into the truly deep and mysterious swirl. While discrimination is real, race is not. The lines—boundaries—between races are illusions with no physical or genetic reality.

Figure 1

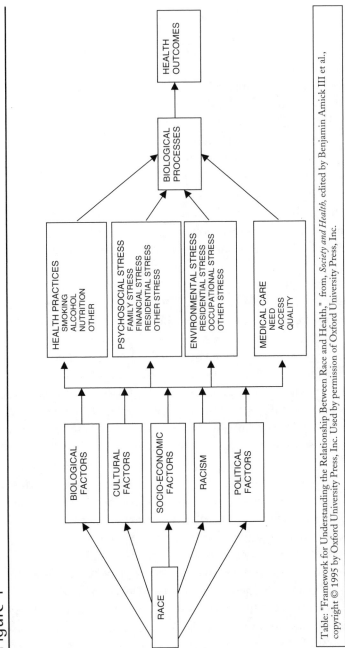

Humans and baboons share about 99 percent of their DNA! How much less the difference between what is called Negroid and Caucasoid, Caucasoid and Mongoloid, Mongoloid and Negroid. Races exist in our minds, which is where racism's effects can do terrible damage over time, and enable all the pathological patterns that link and energize disparities.

Dr. Camara Jones, a researcher with the Centers for Disease Control and Prevention, laid out this argument in a tight presentation to the Morehouse School of Medicine's conference on eliminating disparities in the Southeast. When people say they are measuring race as a determinant associated with health, she notes, they are making race a proxy for some combination of socioeconomic status, culture, and genetics, even though it turns out to be a very rough association in all three areas.

The first link, between race and poverty, is obviously flawed. While blacks are disproportionately represented among the poor, most poor people in the United States are white and many blacks are not poor. Race is not the same as poverty, although they are not entirely different, either: 22 percent of black kids living in poverty have high levels of lead in their blood (which is linked to a web of life-span mental and physical disabilities). Six percent of rich black kids face lead poisoning. But the disease threatens only 2 percent of wealthy white children.

Neither does race stand for culture. As Dr. Jones points out, "There is no one black culture, just as there is no one white culture, Hispanic culture, or Asian culture. In fact, while Ethiopians, Haitians, and African Americans from the rural South might all be labeled 'blacks,' they would all have very different health beliefs and dietary practices."[8]

Race is more difficult to understand as genetic. Blacks in the United States are a genetic admixture of geographic stocks from all over the world, as are whites in this country. When researchers have studied the distribution of genes in populations by ABO blood type, for example, they find an overwhelming variability within a racial group and a small amount of variability between groups. In addition, these genetic markers do not travel together in little "racial packages." The pie slice that we call "race" does not capture genetic variability.

> Race is a precise measure of the social classification of people in our race-conscious society, where that social classification results in profound differences in life experiences and life opportunities. The race that an epidemiologist might note on a study, or that a physician notes in a clinical record, is the same race noted by a police officer, a taxi driver, or a judge in a courtroom. And it is that race that then results in differences in life experiences in this country. Race is a fluid, social construct that is variable between countries and within countries over time. Race is a rough proxy for socioeconomic status, culture, and genetics, but a precise measure of a race system in a race-conscious society.[9]

So why are the patients of a public health doctor like my friend Mike Heisler predictably sickened so often by diseases the majority of white Americans either avoid altogether or get much later in life? Why does this vast disparity persist across so many decades? The linking determinant is racism, functioning over time on three levels: interpersonal, institutional, and internalized.[10] All three work across time intentionally and unintentionally, consciously and unconsciously, to shape the life outcomes of people.

Interpersonal racism uses the criterion of race to make assumptions about the abilities, motives, and intents of others by race, and then responds according to those basic presumptions. For instance, the treatment blacks receive from police, judges, realtors, professors, and physicians (even when both are black) is different from that received by whites. Every black male friend of mine has stories of being stopped by police for "random" checks; of being mistaken as menial help in a hotel; of being questioned on the way to the bathroom by a restaurant owner who fears he is "skipping" without paying; of being shown low-price houses in "black" neighborhoods when searching for a new home. In interpersonal racism, there is always a face to the offense, a person who is making the racist assumption. This blatant racism is easy to recognize, for most of us, at one time or another, participate in it. Multiple negative links to health (and obviously to many other ways of measuring quality of life) result within our society, ranging from outright denial of needed services to chronic "low level" stress for the recipients of such prejudice.

It is a mistake to see this interpersonal level of racism as functioning purely through individual choice, as if racist behaviors simply reflected bad manners or poor choices. This is a boundary mistake often made by those examining the effects of disease on black health. A few researchers, however, have learned not to make this mistake. They have recently been exploring racial disparities in the larger context of social and economic determinants of health (that little bump you felt was another couple of boundaries slipping past). What they now understand as collectively true about those who experience racism represents a major breakthrough in scientific thinking. Discrimination (whether against races or ethnicities or females or homosexuals or elderly or teenagers) can—and does—influence disease processes through a number of potential pathways. While it remains hard to draw exact links between individuals and groups, it is beyond doubt those links exist.

Thus science pushes us toward our second level of racism: institutionalized racism. In U.S. society, it is hard (impossible?) not to be aware that access to goods, services, and opportunities is influenced, and often determined, by race. This racism has no identifiable perpetrator; it is sustained in (and by) our laws, customs, and practices. The result is very different acquisition of material possessions and access to power. There may be no particular face—no pointed white hoods, no red Nazi armbands— around this sort of racism. My father was a man known for his kindness, but he accepted the institutionalized lines of color with all their subconscious protections of benefit and reward, blame and justification. I cannot imagine that they do not echo in my bones too.

Institutionalized racism is usually difficult to see in one's own setting, at least as one on top looks down. Paul Farmer, a Harvard physician and researcher who practices about half the year among the poor in central Haiti, comments:

> We [physicians] learn about pathophysiology, but never the embodiment of the social forces that set in motion a series of events leading, ultimately, to a critical somatic process—hemoptysis due to tuberculosis, say, or the ravaging of the distal small intestine by the bacterium that causes typhoid. And yet most physicians would concede that hunger and a lack of potable water are the root causes of these two diseases.
>
> We are only now beginning to understand the mechanisms by which social inequality is in and of itself pathogenic.[11]

Farmer pushes us beyond artificial boundaries between nations that, he suggests, trap us in "immodest claims of causality." "One of Haiti's lessons for social medicine is that social conditions will to a large extent determine patterns of morbidity and mortality, and that the strength of this association is amplified as conditions worsen."[12]

But why? In framing his answer, Farmer does not ignore his clinical practice devoted to providing medical care to the poor. But his diagnosis includes institutional sickness: "When one of our patients was tortured to death, we attempted to trace the chain of command. It led directly back to U.S. foreign policy: those individuals who had tortured our patient, or ordered him to be tortured, were trained, clothed, and funded by U.S. military aid." Thus this "sudden increase in village-level mortality"—one man tortured to death—was not understandable without a systemic analysis that included the recognition and analysis of international economic and political ties that were and remain linked to the health status of the poor.[13]

Farmer makes the critical move of the boundary leader when he pursues "But why?" out of the too-small container of the phenomenon. The container of nationality is inappropriate; it obscures like a fog. Likewise, the container of time is often inappropriate, as if that which came before, the past, should be—or can ever be—left out of the picture. Farmer thinks at the scale of the system affecting his patients and follows the threads of lives and health across boundaries into the boundary zone.

The third kind of racism, internalized, describes the values and outlooks within—deep inside—the person as he or she integrates negative assumptions of subordination and oppression. Such dehumanizing "self-devaluation" is evident in many common occurrences; an example is black-on-black crime: "If a person does not value himself," writes Camara Jones, "then he will not value others who look like him."[14] Resignation, helplessness, and hopelessness are all factors of internalized racism that turn into unhealthy behaviors: cigarette smoking, substance abuse, violent acts, and so on.

Dr. Fred Smith is professor of Urban Ministries at Wesley Seminary in Washington, D.C., and pastor of a church in Ambridge, Pennsylvania, down the river from Pittsburgh. The city is not "at risk"; it already *is* road kill on the highway from industrial devolution. Fred knows all three levels of racism that Jones identifies and adds a fourth she does not quite reach. He grew up in the Oakland projects, went on a football scholarship to Harvard (first in his family to go to any college at all), then did graduate work at Southern Methodist University and Emory University. His dissertation, "Without a Vision: A Functional Theological Proposal for a Prophetic Christian Education for Black Boys," explores the pathology of internalized racism in which

the lack of a strong sense of coherence among African American males in particular and marginalized people in general is the result of the confusion of double-consciousness, which refers to double aims that divide the spiritual self, making the environment incomprehensible. The social self is confounded by a triple quandary of a hegemonic socialization process that impacts the meaningfulness of life. The internalization of the hegemonic intentions of socializing institutions results in the internalization oppression that leads to nihilism.[15]

Fred never speaks for long about his life without talking about his nephew Hasaan, who died by gunfire on the same streets Fred walked years before. Hasaan was the family's next great hope, a young man with the potential to follow Fred to college and into a profession. After Hasaan's death, Fred wrote a letter to his young friends in the old neighborhood.

I am very afraid for you, because I know that many of you looked up to Hasaan and will try to follow in his path. The street Hasaan died on is the street my friends and I used to walk day and night singing the Temptations' greatest hits without fear. We made money on that street throwing papers and returning Coke bottles to the corner store. Now kids are selling dope on that same corner. We fought with fists instead of guns. We planned our futures and not our funerals.

Your ancestors learned a long time ago that we are a small minority in this country, but that did not stop them from struggling for their freedom against all odds. Our forefathers struggled for freedom from physical chains enforced by whips and hunting dogs. Your father's father struggled for freedom from legal and political chains enforced by terror and the lynching tree. Your father fought for civil rights against segregation enforced by Jim Crow laws, for voting rights, equal opportunity, and affirmative action. You must fight to stay alive, to escape from bullets instead of plantations, and you must break the bonds of mind-numbing drugs instead of chains of iron.

Many black boys today believe they have no future. . . . Live fast, die young, and have a pretty corpse is the logic of the terminally ill. This is the greatest challenge you will face—to keep hope alive. Every day, I am shocked and bewildered by the coldheartedness of killing that takes place in our neighborhoods at the hands of young brothers 11, 12, and 13. But I guess if you don't care about your own life why should you care about anyone else.

No one can long endure without love, so some of you turn to gangs that become your family. You are on the right track. But does your adopted family create or destroy community? Is your new family held together by love or fear? If you are to find meaning, hope, and love in your life, you must seek to live in peace with all your brothers—not just those who wear your colors. Because your fight is "not against flesh and blood [as Paul wrote to the Ephesians twenty centuries ago] but against principalities, against powers, against rulers of the darkness of this world, against spiritual wickedness in high places." Your struggle is against . . . the violence itself.[16]

Fred helps us see that the three levels of racism are more like dimensions of a living phenomenon than separate and distinct components of a mechanical system. The fourth aspect of it is that it is alive, a beast in which we live and which lives inside us. As a boundary leader, Fred follows the path that others fear into the boundary zone with all its terrible brokenness. Freed from the false simplicities, he can see clearly enough to lament deeply and fully for what is lost. But at the root of the grief, he finds a surprising hope that is just as tenacious and resilient. Life is still there to be chosen.

Profile: Romie Lilly

It is impossible to be in two places at one time. But Romie Lilly comes close.

His title at Central Baptist Church in Englewood, California, is "Community Convener." The community includes the four hundred members of this African American congregation, the people of South Central Los Angeles, the people of Los Angeles County, the state of California, and anybody willing to lessen the gaping disparities in health care and justice that afflict far too many people.

The story of his ministry is peppered with the perceptions of his community, each followed by the words "Just last week," or "I just got back from a demonstration," or "I've just been appointed" to one board or another that is bound and determined to bring about change. If Romie has anything to say about it, he will awaken a sleeping city.

"This past Friday I held a session on domestic violence," Lilly recalls. "We pulled together people from media to see how we might frame the issue to make it work for everyone. I have relationships in the faith community and in the media. One of the things that has restricted progress is that oftentimes the minority community feels left behind. We don't set the agenda and so we feel trapped by the language of other folks."

Reframing issues is an essential part of Lilly's style. Take domestic violence. Lilly noted a media group's study that while gang violence is reported in the media regularly, domestic violence cases are virtually invisible. "There is not enough outrage about this," Lilly says.

The inequitable coverage of racial violence also appalls Lilly. "Three years ago, a white family made a wrong turn in East Los Angeles and got shot. Everybody was outraged. But in the six months prior to that, twelve Latinos were killed—there was little outrage about that. Reframing these issues is really my mission."

"This work demands that you have a strategy. You have to sit down and take time, real time, to develop a strategy that includes language and perceptions. And then you work out how you are going to target it. If you rush in with emotion, you might be right at first but you miss the point because you didn't have the strategy. We need both the results and the emotion."

To combat the devastation of gang violence, "we had an initiative that deals with children's deaths by firearms. We called that 'Not Even One.' 'Not Even One' child's death by firearms is acceptable or inevitable. The death of a child in this way is not 'normative', it is unacceptable behavior." Lilly's strategy is not to "run up saying, 'I've got the best idea'. Instead, we're saying, 'Let's see what really happened'. If we find some commonalities, then maybe we devise programs to prevent" such things as drive-by shootings.

To help reframe issues, Romie turns to Scripture in an unusual way. He often uses the actions of Jonah, who tried to dodge God's call to witness to the people of the great city of Nineveh. Instead of following God's summons, Jonah ran away.

"People in the church can identify with this book of Jonah," Lilly says. "When we get to a certain point in meetings, we raise a question: Are we going to hesitate and hide? Or are we going to accept our call?"

Then Lilly calls on them to care about the child who is shot *and* the child who pulls the trigger; for the woman who is abused *and* the husband who abuses her. All of this requires training church leaders to acknowledge their own spiritual gifts and to develop strategies that reframe the issues. "Once you get the training, and once you get equipped for leadership, then you get invited to participate," Lilly says.

There is a lot to do. Los Angeles County has been in financial crisis; the county health program skirts on the edge of bankruptcy. Martin Luther King Hospital, the lifeline for the poor, could be closed. Lilly marched with others protesting budget cuts in health services.

"Things are getting worse," Lilly adds. "Fewer and fewer resources are available, and the problems seem insurmountable. Probably due to my faith and the faith of many people, we continue to believe that God is present in what we do, and that presence is important.

"But another thing is happening here. When you are an African American older than fifty, you have seen a lot of stuff go down, and you realize that things aren't as hopeless as they appear to be. Maybe it's the wisdom of age. You know that things can change.

"Many people don't know things can change because they haven't lived long enough to see that happen. So when life gets overwhelming, they despair and high rates of suicide and violence occur.

"The apostle Paul says, 'By my faith I'll show you who I am.' He is not just saying 'I have faith,' but 'Let's talk about the results of what faith has brought you.' African Americans have experienced some pretty awful things, so we have learned, by faith, to see the possibility in the darkest situation . . . the courage not to run and hide, not to deny the ministry of compassion for all God's people.

"It is a resurrection thing."

As the old spiritual hymn says so eloquently,

> We've come this far by faith
> Leaning on the Lord
> Trusting in His Holy Word
> He's never failed yet.
> Oh, can't turn around
> We've come this far by faith.
> Don't be discouraged with trouble in your life
> He'll bear your burdens
> And move all misery and strife.
> That's why we've come this far by faith.[17]

Reframing Race in the Boundary Zones

One focus of the Interfaith Health Program (IHP) of Emory University, where I work, is called the Institute for Public Health and Faith Collaborations. In this program, we seek to build the capacity of teams of leaders to engage disparities in health through collaboration between faith groups and public health institutions. We try to help leaders move toward and through the complexity of the problems so that they can move their communities toward durable transformation.

The essential move in thinking, the initial requirement in generating community wholeness, is to see disparities as a challenge rooted in our social structures that are themselves nurtured by social processes that are sustained by social beliefs and attitudes. This is very deep and turbulent water that erodes the boundaries of organizations and structures that try to engage it. This clearly blows past the narrow lines of authority of the health professions, even the public health professions. As we have seen, most of the causes of the disparities in health are not "health issues," but lie in other fields and even beyond them too. Disparities in health draw leaders toward one another in the boundary zone. We need tools fit for deep water.

"Reframing"—a technique developed by Lee Bolman and Terrence Deal—helps us help organizational managers see their challenges using the full range of perspectives (see figure 2). We flip the perspective inside out to help teams of leaders understand the full breadth of their communities' challenges. This adds a dimension to Jones's concepts of racism and its relationship to enduring health disparities, multiplying leaders' capacity to ask "But why?" in more and more powerful ways.

> The essential move in thinking is to see disparities as a challenge rooted in our social structures that are themselves nurtured by social processes that are sustained by social beliefs and attitudes.

The four frames used in reframing are "structural," which deals with rules and roles, policies and technology; "human resource," which focuses on personnel needs, training, and relationships; "political," which is most interested in power dynamics; and finally, "symbolic," which gives top priority to culture, meaning, and story.

Bolman and Deal note that each of the frames has its own image of reality: the way things really are, and the way things need to be approached. They suggest that each of us tends to use one or two of the frames as our "natural" way of seeing our world. For instance, organizational managers are most comfortable in the structural frame; they analyze, respond, and lead out of that way of understanding their environment and relationships. Each of us will find that "some frames may

Figure 2

Overview of the Four-FrameModel

	Frame			
	Structural	*Human Resource*	*Political*	*Symbolic*
Metaphor for organization	Factory or machine	Family	Jungle	Carnival, temple, theater
Central concepts	Rules, roles, goals, policies, technology, environment	Needs, skills, relation-ships	Power, conflict, competition, organizational politics	Culture, meaning, metaphor, ritual, ceremony, stories, heroes
Image of leadership	Social architecture	Empower-ment	Advocacy	Inspiration
Basic leadership challenge	Attune structure to task, technology, environment	Align organiza-tional and human needs	Develop agenda and power base	Create faith, beauty, meaning

From *Reframing Organization*, Second Edition, Lee Bolman and Terrance Deal, Copyright © 1991, 1996 Jossey-Bass Publishers. Reprinted by permission of John Wiley & Sons, Inc.

Figure 3

Race and the Four-Frame Model

Three Levels of Race	Four Frame of Race			
	Structural	*Human Resource*	*Political*	*Symbolic*
Interpersonal	Relationships reinforced by legal and organizational patterns.	Relationship as taught, trained, rewarded.	Relationship reinforced or manipulated by political discourse, conflict, and public movements.	Relations modeled by iconic leaders, song, in worship, family, and group stories.
Institutional	Racial behavior and response reflects rules, roles, official goals, policies, formal expectations.	Negative or helpful behaviors engaged (or purposefully not) by training and systematic rewards.	Power is engaged using conflict, mediation, negotiation conflict, via politics at all levels of the human systems.	Public stories, symbols, official occasions used to reinforce or change meanings.
Internalized	Personal goals and life expectations reflect analysis of institutional architecture. Shapes sense of risk, hope, vulnerability.	Caculation of value of types of education, mentors, and personal experiences shape self-understanding.	Participation in public, systemic, political change strategies shape self-perception, trust, sense of efficacy and resilience.	Identification with leaders, role models. Relevance of suffering vs. liberating Jesus, or distrust of all theology.

seem clear and straightforward while others seem puzzling." The point is not that one or another frame is "right," but that as we learn to use all four, we "should develop greater appreciation and deeper understanding" of organizations. When Galileo devised the first telescope, he discovered that each lens he added contributed to a more accurate image of the heavens. Successful managers take advantage of the same truth. They reframe until they bring the situation at hand into clear focus.[18] The purpose of the whole concept of the frames is oriented toward helping the manager know what to do— closer to our question of "So what?" than "But why?"

Used within the context of our discussion of racism, the four frames allow us to follow the "But why?" of disparities much further into the boundary zone. My "reframing" on the left may look different from a version you would do (see figure 3), but either mine or one you create from your own experiences should begin to offer some answers to what to do and the kind of relationships among leaders that we will need.

Translating Bolman and Deal's frames of reference into our language of boundaries helps us comprehend and conquer limiting and confining borders. Institutionalized racism, now graphically delineated and therefore easier to see, can be followed around and outside the walls of traditional boxes. A boundary leader's first instinct is to go right to the edge of any frame and look beyond it. The four frames offer a whole new set of tools that bring possibilities into view that would otherwise remain murky and muddled.

An internal manager uses the frames to look inside, but any boundary leader knows the outside is what matters: the organization is seldom the appropriate container for any subject worth thinking about. How could race and disparities ever be contained within any organization? The four frames help launch the "But why?" and the "So what?" outward, across any boundary that threatens to contain the search.

In engaging the institutional form of racism, Paul Farmer follows political questions about "But why?" in ways that allow him to see Haiti and the United States as one pathologically coherent system. He uses all four frames, but finds special power in critical questions about "development," which has worked to shield external economic interests from criticism. Exposing their hypocritical affects, Farmer works in the symbolic frame to rip the illusion to shreds.

Farmer follows patients to their homes, for example, where he finds that their brutal existence is partly a result of being displaced by a hydroelectric dam built in the name of development. Now the power plant provides electricity to the capital city, leaving the people from villages that were flooded to scrap like animals, deprived not only of their traditional methods of livelihood but also of their history and certainly of their future. He explores the structural implications of providing public health programs to this pillaged people; indeed, he tries to offer the same quality of medical services to his patients in Haiti and at Harvard. He is well known for using the symbolic frame of analysis and action—"But why?" and "So what?"—among policy makers and public health colleagues around the world.

Camara Jones does the same; in fact, she first presented her framework of racism at a conference designed to help physicians and policy makers understand what they could do—in concert with community partners—to eliminate disparities in the southeastern United States. She destroys the simplistic illusions about racism and replaces them with analytical tools fit for the complex boundary zone environment in which race can be engaged with adult commitment.

Once you know you are in the boundary zone, you look for other tools that fit the challenge. Ronald Heifetz and Donald Laurie, like Bolman and Deal, have worked extensively with companies facing complex management challenges. They give us a helpful distinction between *technical* and *adaptive* challenges.

A technical problem is one for which we expect someone to provide a definitive answer. There are *some* problems like that inside organizations, although the pace of technological and organizational change makes them harder and harder to find.

An adaptive challenge, on the other hand, results when "our deeply held beliefs are challenged, when the values that made us successful become less relevant, and when legitimate yet competing perspectives emerge."[19] Adaptive work is different from technical work—more stressful, emotionally draining—because one is not certain what the answer will even look like when it is found, or when it might be found, or who might find it. Many boundary leaders are technical kinds of thinkers who have been drawn by their relationships into the adaptive work of boundary zones. What differs and distinguishes them from other managers is that they have learned no longer to think of offering "technical assistance" to organizations and leaders. They know what is really needed is "adaptive assistance"—tools fit for adaptive work.

An example of the shift needed to rescue adaptive reasoning from technical stalemate comes from my friend Bill Bolling, who, at the time of this story—the early 1970s—was assistant pastor of St. Luke's Episcopal Church in downtown Atlanta.

Bill one day notices hungry people coming by to ask for food: a technical problem. Bill then notices that the church secretary is in the habit of bringing a few extra peanut butter sandwiches with her to work: a technical solution to the recurrent problem. Bill's response is not to build, as it were, a bigger and better sandwich. He follows instead the thread of those requests logically to create what he understands to be a mega-, but still technical, solution: a food bank that could systematically collect and distribute the bountiful wasted food available from donors (if you would just ask) and make them available to the many other churches and social service organizations faced with people needing food.

Thirty years later the Metro Atlanta Community Food Bank collects and distributes millions of pounds of food every year through nearly a thousand nonprofit organizations. It is an integral part of the food system in the state of Georgia.

But that is not all it is: today it is also an advocate for the poor and hungry. Its work combines multiple technical innovations with an adaptive orientation to the community. The food bank is the home of a dozen adaptive coalitions, notably dealing with homelessness, the working poor, and regional leadership. Whenever any issue touching the lives of the poor surfaces in Atlanta and Georgia, the Food Bank has usually created a space for the voice of the poor to be heard.

Once we know we are in the boundary zone we not surprised by complexity, even if we do not have good language to describe it. We are like farmers gone to sea or sailors gone to farming: the precision of our language is useless to describe the environment in which we live *now*. It helps to know that boundary zones have three peculiar dimensions: scale, time, and adaptivity.

The first dimension is scale: How many people along the "hunger" continuum are affected? At one end is the unlucky aberrant individual; at the other is the nearly permanent group—a collection of unlucky aberrant individuals—experiencing a pattern of disparity: in total, millions of families in thousands of communities across continents.

The second dimension is time: How durable is the problem? Here we find at one end the unforeseen, single-stroke crisis with no local precedent: homeless man dies in a blizzard (open a shelter!). At the other end is an enduring pattern across generations, nations, and projecting into the future: millions of homeless who face death and danger as a result of a lifestyle that has been forced upon them by societal unconcern.

The third dimension is adaptivity: Do we know what to do? At one end of the continuum lie apparent problems of finance: people do not have enough money to buy clothes (start a thrift shop!). At the other end lie challenges that are integral to the fabric of global social, political, and economic patterns. Again, disparities—often racial, but including other prejudices and neglect, too—create conditions in which lack of clothing, food, and shelter is more a symptom than a cause. Here patterns are more than material, more than human. They are spiritual in the sense that they embody a reality that is all-inclusive.

Any conceivable problem or opportunity lies somewhere along this three-dimensional continuum. Almost no problem lies all the way at one end, with no accent of the other tension. Even the most obvious technical problem has some aspect of adaptivity on the horizon. (Keeping the church mailing list? Hmmm. Rolodex or Palm Pilot . . . why not on the Web?) Even the most obvious swarm of related adaptive challenges—racial disparities in health—has multiple embedded challenges and opportunities that contain technical elements (genetic mapping, housing and health patterns, social epidemiology possible only with recent computer power). It helps to see the challenges on a continuum so that you can use the full assets that fit reality.

What makes the boundary zone the environment that it is, is that all of these levels and dimensions function in a constantly shifting and dynamically complex system—much more complex than three levels this way, and four the next. Farmer and Jones, Bolman and Deal, Heifetz and Laurie, all stretch us into multiple dimensions. But understand: their models point toward greater complexity than their descriptions.

Boundary zones create leaders able to risk asking open-ended questions of the whole system, then able to imagine responses that are consistent with those answers (which will lead us toward other questions . . .).

Is it possible to think and act at the level of the system of disparities? Is it possible to move *systematically* in the boundary zone?

One example of a coalition doing this very thing is the Minnesota Health Improvement Partnership. In April 2001 the partnership issued a "call to action." After an extensive series of town meetings and systematic analysis of Minnesota health patterns, the partnership found that the state ranks as one of the healthiest in the nation, but there remain significant groups of its citizens who experience poor health decade after decade. A simple vision—"all people in Minnesota have an equal opportunity to enjoy good health"—drew the partnership into a detailed and carefully enunciated 96-page plan for "advancing health for all through social and economic change."[20] The report was drafted by the partnership's "social conditions and health action team," which noted in the executive summary: *"These findings challenge us to change the way we implement health improvement efforts, examine the health impact of social and economic forces at play outside the traditional health sector, and renew attention to the roles we play as individuals and organizations in creating and perpetuating these disparities."*

The report begins with an expansive definition of health that crosses about a dozen boundaries: "Health is more than not being sick. Health is a resource for everyday life—the ability to realize hopes, satisfy needs, change or cope with life experiences, and participate fully in society. Health has physical, mental, social, and spiritual dimensions."

Most of the report is filled with detailed recommendations—things that fall into our "So what?" category—that range from adaptive steps to increase social capital and social cohesion, to nitty-gritty technical details that will make state department of health grants more accessible to community organizations.

The partnership recognizes that new mechanisms to deliver funding must be developed that balance accountability with maximum flexibility, community autonomy, and efficiency. Nevertheless, says the partnership's report, because the Minnesota Department of Health operates numerous grant programs, it is in a position to take immediate steps that will begin a long-term process of reorienting funding by:

- involving a greater variety of people in evaluating grant proposals
- notifying more community-based organizations from around the state of the availability of grants
- streamlining administrative requirements

- determining barriers to funding initiatives designed to eliminate disparities
- requiring that grant applicants involve community-based organizations and/or representatives from the populations to be served in the preparation of the grant proposal, and in the implementation of the grant.

The report imagines a long journey to justice that needs a great deal more analysis, research, listening, stories, and evaluation of initiatives and time. But the journey is already underway.

Gloria Lewis, director of the Office of Minority Health of Minnesota, was among the boundary leaders who attended IHP's Institute for Public Health and Faith Collaborations. She frequently slipped out of the intense discussions inside the room to take calls from legislators who wanted to question funding for the initiative. In the end the funding (for 2003) was held constant with 2002's amounts.

Lewis describes the work as a movement, which she defines as "that force that carries you—that moves you—to places you would not imagine going otherwise."

Minnesota is in the boundary zone of disparities and knows it. More precisely, the Social Conditions and Health Action Team of the Minnesota Health Improvement Partnership knows it. I would guess that a lot more Minnesotans know about the Mall of America out near the Minneapolis airport than know about disparities in health among their fellow citizens.

This is not a small point. Will our boundary zone strategies work?

The Minnesota model raises the issue of the relationship of boundary leaders not just to the boundary zones, but to one another. The form of their relationship, the webs of transformation, is the subject of a later chapter. But the nature of those relationships grows from the nature of the boundary zones, so it is crucial to make the immediate link. Boundary leaders find themselves drawn into the complex system of communities that are boundary zones—beyond the technical and into the adaptive—and, once inside, they discover that the relationships that emerge are like the boundary zones themselves: unpredictable, surprising, fraught with possibilities. All the boundary leaders in this book have stories of surprising relationships that emerge as they move ahead on what might have seemed a lonely walk. The irony is that the willingness to move alone creates the possibility of new relationships that both confirm and transform us on the way. Traditional "leaders" see the chaos of community and lean toward defense (building walls, constructing barriers) or—even more foolishly—attack (breaking through others' boundaries). They judge themselves by whether they add to the capacity of a group to defend itself from a perceived threat. Boundary leaders, on the other hand, do not think in terms of defense and "security." They lose the illusion of security and exchange it for a new kind of assurance that resonates in relationships fit for the boundary zones. Given tools to understand, focus, frame, describe, and systematically engage the most highly contentious phenomenon— even race—boundary leaders are fit for their task. One last surprise remains.

Into the Boundary Zones and Back to Home

Race and its inevitably deadly disparities is a boundary zone phenomenon that illuminates the crucial nature of all boundary zone issues: You do not go somewhere else to engage it— you realize you are in it already. The boundary zone is not a domain removed in time from the present, as if we can go there when we are ready, remain here until we are prepared. It is where we are. Now. The challenges of the boundary zone are not in front of us. They are in between us, around us, among us: between and among and around our structures, existing relationships, organizations, networks, groups.

A boundary zone is the space in between the structures, organizations, and groups. We do not *go there*, actually, because *we are there already*. As Jones, Farmer, Smith, and the Minnesota boundary leaders articulate so clearly, that space is filled with fields of relationship, with powerful histories that bind us together, some of which we acknowledge, much of which we only dimly perceive, some of which we resist knowing at all. Those relationships are almost impossible to see when you think the world is made up of contiguous nation-states, organizations, companies, congregations, schools, disciplines, guilds, tribes, races, clubs, and all the other names we give to the identities we think define and contain us. When you follow the thread of "But why?" and "So what?" the membrane between those identities breaks down, dissolves, and melts away. We find those threads of relationships tangle in awkward and hopeful ways that disregard the sovereignty of all those passing identities. The boundary zone is that space where things touch and engage in surprising ways, ways that disturb the content and encourage those folk who are restless and hopeful for change.

> **The most powerful function of boundary leadership is to change the relationships between the humans involved in the systems.**

The old ways of knowing who we are and how we are related are melting away. New ways of relating are emerging. Chaos theory suggests that when a system moves far enough from its old equilibrium or stable state, it either dissipates or it moves to a new, more complex form of order. The lens of disparities suggests that our social and political systems are facing a crisis of self-knowledge that undermines all the old ideas of patient progress trickling down over time. The same crisis born of deep grief and powerful hope is visible in other major movements surging throughout time.

Bill McKibben wrote a book in 1990 titled *The End of Nature*.[21] In it he documented that the lines we once imagined existing between the natural and human world are totally gone. We once thought that nature was big and slow to change; our human efforts were small and fragile. Sometime too recent for us to notice or believe, the relationship changed; we now know our largest planetary systems are profoundly impacted by cumulative human action—some purposeful and stupid, some unintentional and stupid. McKibben knows there is one boundary zone and that we are all in it. There is no boundary between anything that matters on this tiny spinning rock we call home.

I look up from my computer through the window to a high Appalachian ridge whose beauty stuns me. My eyes take in the light shifting across the folded land. I can see only one other home across the green canopy. But I know that a bear standing on the far ridge tonight will see the aurora of lights from the new Wal-Mart a dozen miles south toward Atlanta. Perhaps better than most of the neighboring mammals— humans especially—the bear knows we are living beyond any boundaries that matter. We are living in one common space: the boundary zone.

So what? Does it make any difference to see things this way? Do we gain anything of substance and value by flipping all our conceptual frameworks upside down and inside out? I think so. The most powerful function of boundary leadership is to change the relationships between the humans involved in the systems. They do not bring any new, much less unique, technical solutions. But the relationships they weave function like a kind of scaffolding from which the most technical solutions can be brought to bear on the problems. As an old carpenter, I know that sometimes the hardest part of the job is building the scaffolding that makes it possible to do what most people think of as the "real work".

Profile: *Tor Haugstad*

For years, public health has been a secular concern. This is especially true in Norway, where the church, once responsible for health care, in the past century has yielded healing to the scientific and technological communities and has withdrawn to the "spiritual" world. Yet research reveals that faith does influence health. So Dr. Tor Haugstad, a neurologist who teaches at the University of Oslo, has been working to bring the two communities—faith and health—together for discussion. It is an effort reflecting concepts that have been forming his entire life.

"I was born in India in 1951 and grew up there," Haugstad explains. "My mother was a missionary doctor, my father a pastor with the Norwegian Lutheran missionary agency. We worked in leprosy colonies northeast of Calcutta. My parents pushed boundaries in their own lives." It was logical, Haugstad reflects, that he developed "a notion that church and health were closely linked."

At one mission station, the Haugstads arrived to find only "five or six baptized Christians and no congregations at all." When they left ten years later, there were seventy congregations and more than one thousand baptized Christians. "Many of these people came to believe in Christ," Haugstad recalls, "because they came to the mission hospital when they were sick and they saw the dedication and they heard the songs and the prayers. They came to understand that the driving force of my parents' lives was the love of the sole God of the universe who sent his Son to heal creation. A God who cares for sick people and weak people, and people engulfed in sin and shame—that was very surprising for them. They became part of the church."

Lepers were outcasts who needed not only medical treatment but also attention and acceptance. It took an "outside community" to bring about change. Early in his life, Haugstad recognized the blessing, and the tension, inherent in cross-cultural situations. "I learned that the driving force was love of the world," he says.

At first he planned to be a medical missionary. But his call became clearer as he studied medicine. "I've been a physician in Norway my entire career." But he has never left the church. Even while a medical student, he would relax from his studies by slipping away to the church, where he played Bach or Mozart or Handel on the organ. An accomplished organist, he continues to find peace and beauty in music.

The cross-cultural experiences of his youth have helped him understand the relationships between nations and people, he says. "It has given me a kind of understanding of people in totally different cultures and settings. I realized we should really learn to reach out to each other."

A recent interest has been the problem of migration. "We have a lot of Asians and Africans coming to Norway, and they struggle to get adjusted. This was the challenge I too had when I moved back to Norway. It was supposed to be my home, but I had a hard time understanding what my fellow students were talking about. We have a lot of people coming to Norway from Pakistan and Sudan and Morocco, and I sort of see what kinds of difficulties they are having."

The dialogue between church and healing that he had seen so clearly in his parents became increasingly important in his life. "When I was in medical school, I realized that medicine in Europe had its roots in monasteries, which were also the hospitals in medieval times. The church had been split very far from medicine. But I had seen this connection growing up. In fact, most of the hospitals in India were run by mission organizations.

"But hospitals were not perceived that way in Norway," Haugstad continues. "The government took care of health and the church was not involved at all. How had we drifted so far apart? Why do we not relate to each other?"

To pursue those questions, Haugstad initiated a series of dialogues and conversations with the Ministry of Health. "In 1996, I was part of writing a church report to the Ministry of Health. It was incorporated into a parliamentary bill. They decided that the church should start collaborating again, and that there should be an ongoing dialogue on the national level. So we have conferences every year with top church and government leaders. The minister of health has said that the church needs to discuss the basic values of medicine and health care, and that it must discuss the priorities. How much should we spend to understand disease? How much do we spend to care for the afflicted? How much do we try and cure, and how much work do we do on a social level in public health? And how do we strategize while taking care of young children, and cancer patients, people with strokes, and those suffering from Alzheimer's? There has never been a high level reflection on all of this; instead these decisions have been made in a haphazard way. It must be a moral, not just a utilitarian, discussion."

Similar discussions are beginning in other countries as well. Haugstad and the Interfaith Health Program are creating a network of centers around the globe to explore how religious values can be useful in the public health arena. The focus may be economic assets, or health institutions, or hospitals, or ministries of health, but in each case the basic questions are repeated: What good can be done? And by what means?

"The concept of boundary leadership is being practiced in Norway," Haugstad says. "The Norwegian Minister of Health has a personal church background, so he immediately understood that the church could contribute to health issues. He suggested that churches institute an 'All Sorrows Day' to focus on patients who felt they were not being well treated or were not satisfied with their lives. We haven't gotten very far, but I am struck with how on-target some of these health officials have been.

"To me, this is very meaningful. Although I was never a missionary abroad, I am becoming a missionary at home as I try to talk with both church and health leaders, trying to come up with ideas on how we can be useful. I think they are quite pleased with this."

Scripture has always been an inspiration in Haugstad's life. Recently, the Gospel of John has taken on special meaning.

"The book's author is called the apostle of love," Haugstad says. "That love is not just a feeling. It is not something that we express in words, but love is an action, a practice. John's whole point is that God so loved the world that he sent his Son, and this is how we are to be. Love is how we live out relationships. Love is reaching out to the afflicted, to people in sorrow and pain."

Haugstad believes "the future is entirely in God's hands." That does not mean that human beings have no role in bringing God's plan into fruition. "In the end, John writes, all of the evil is defeated, and a new world is revealed," Haugstad says. "So my task is to be part of this battle against the evil things and all of the bad things that can happen—diseases and war. I have to do what I can, but the victory is not in my hands, it is in God's hands."

3

Boundary Leaders

*The goal before us is to understand complexity. . . . We must move
beyond structure and topology and start focusing on the dynamics
that take place along the links. Networks are only the skeleton of
complexity, the highways for various processes that make our work
hum. To describe society we must dress the links of the social network
with the actual dynamical interactions between people.*

Albert-László Barabási, *Linked*

Who Are They?

Millicent moves toward the pictures on the wall with reverence, slowly, as she might move toward an altar. A strong black
woman licensed to preach at age 47 after an administrative
career in the state mental health system of Louisiana, she
moves with authority, confident in her calling to bless. We are
silent, our thoughts carried by the keyboard, where Bill
Chaney does a jazz riff on "How Great Thou Art."

Only Millicent thinks to bless. She weaves though and
among us, reaching out and gently touching each of our

drawings—our crudely drawn mosaics, our quickly sketched quilts: eyes closed, she prays, blesses, each one of them.

How does she know we need her blessing? Or that we deserve it?

Millicent is one of forty boundary leaders meeting at a retreat center on the banks of the Mississippi River. We each have drawn a montage: pictures of our family, of ourselves in some leadership role, of our community. Displayed before us, they form a tapestry of personal complexity. Most of the drawings are crude, put together in thirty minutes. But they are also creative acts of intentional transparency and disclosure, exposure and revelation, hanging boldly on white lattice room dividers for all to see.

Quilt drawing is an exercise at each of these events sponsored by Interfaith Health Program. The sharing of ourselves is always a sacred moment. But until Millicent, no one had done the obvious thing: honored our gifts of self with a spirit of prayer and reverence. On one quilt a woman has pasted a family snapshot onto which she has sketched with her ballpoint pen a picture of her deceased husband—still very much in her life, if not capable of being captured on film. Children: young, old, dead and still grieved, crowd other drawings. Communities in tatters; churches founded by grandfathers; pictures of pets. And more children. Many write Bible verses and favorite quotations as frames to look through, as lenses to keep the images in focus.

The boundary leaders gathered here from Georgia, California, Texas, Louisiana, and Missouri are a mixed lot of religious and public community leaders. But to look into their job descriptions would miss the point. Rather we look to learn how they see themselves, especially their self-perceived weaknesses and strengths.

Over the thirty years I have been on the learning curve of community change, I have come to recognize a pattern among those drawn to the boundaries. In 1998 I interviewed twenty-eight people who responded to a paragraph describing the idea of boundary leaders. All were involved in community work;

about two-thirds of them worked for a public agency, the balance for religious groups. Since then, similar studies have reinforced my findings, notably those described in the books *Cultural Creatives* and *Common Fire.*[1] All of us were wondering, Who *are* these people drawn to where the future can be envisioned: contested, tattered, in pieces, but still vital?

I call them "boundary leaders" because the term gives a positive twist to the pejorative, self-deprecating ways many tend to describe themselves. They often underestimate their power and overestimate their weakness. In both perceptions—of weakness and strength—they accept the perspective and hierarchical models of the business and/or organization world, much as a minority culture will internalize the negative perceptions of the dominant culture. Some of what seems to them weakness may, indeed, be weakness. But in many cases (in my experience, in most cases) their characteristic pattern of strength and weakness makes boundary leaders well suited to the work and demands of the boundary zone. In that social ecology, traditional organizational attitudes and outlooks adapt poorly; they weaken one's ability to face—and to conquer—the particular challenges of the boundaries.

Known but Unknown

Because they work on the margins, it is not surprising that boundary leaders describe themselves as marginal. They are often out of sight, literally as well as figuratively, of the central office. They see themselves as living on the side, out of the way, unnoticed by those clustered in the heart of their organizations. Boundary leaders frequently describe themselves as being invisible. Their organizations, they believe, tend to forget them. Even when they work for a small church or a small community agency with little "inside" to demand their time, they feel their work outside those walls is not seen, much less valued. They are not taken into account and then they are thought to be unaccountable in the normal organizational arithmetic.

Boundary leaders tend to have many "thin" relationships: their working relationships may be many, but often these are shallow, not grounded deeply enough for intimacy or trust. One woman, pastor of a small Lutheran congregation in a small North Dakota town, lamented: "Nobody ever told me I would be lonely among so many conversations. I am always moving from one to the other, but I am almost unknown, really."

The nature of their work outside the office walls—in community—makes many boundary leaders unknown, or barely known, back at headquarters. Relationships there seldom mature from acquaintances to friendships. As one public health worker from Texas noted, "Boundary leader people are pretty lonely, and if you don't have a few friends to help nurture you, friends to just talk to and who can understand you when you talk, it's very hard." Another reflected that despite their many relationships, boundary leaders need "an ability to stand alone. In fact I think standing alone, that ability to stand alone and not take offense, is major."

Ironically, boundary leaders have so extensive a network that others seek them out to connect people to one another. But the thin nature of those many relationships means boundary leaders themselves know and are known by few people very well.

The wounds suffered on the edges differ from those at the core. The main office is a dangerous environment too, but the threats are more predictable and avoidable. Deep inside the organization, one may be pale from lack of sunlight, flabby from lack of activity. Not so in the boundary zones, where there are broken and jagged edges to dodge, openings and opportunities to discover. In most urban areas, you can trip (quite literally) over bodies sleeping on the streets. Any urban boundary leader knows where *not* to step, but that knowledge itself can become scar tissue hiding old psychic wounds. I can still remember the first time I noticed someone sleeping on the doorsteps of a downtown Baptist church I had driven by a thousand times. I am sad to say that I am never surprised by that all-too-frequent sight anymore, but that ease is another kind of wound.

In *Common Fire*, the authors analyzed the personal and financial costs experienced by those I call boundary leaders. Their interviewees had sustained lifetime commitments, which are exceptional for people working in such difficult, traditionally burn-out circumstances. But the invariable result was less pay and fewer promotions—and more stress—than they might have earned trodding safer paths. The stress was personal, but also familial: spouses and children who share their loved ones with the world. "People of color in our sample, particularly the African Americans, revealed a significant measure of ill health. . . . [A] disproportionate number had suffered early stroke, cancer, and death since the interviews."[2] In "serving as bridges between two worlds," these boundary leaders experience "the loneliness" and pain of "endless and constant translation." Boundary leaders, who are likely to spend a lot of time transcending race and culture, always have to translate the value of their labor outside the perimeter of normal organizational standards: "If your job were important, it would be down here at the office."

Inside the walls of organizations, one may be subverted or marginalized by familiar political scheming and manipulation. In the boundary zone, it is more likely that one is hurt by careless arrogance, the thoughtless collateral damage of power exerted in low-value spaces. Without the organization's shelter, those in the boundary zones are exposed. Their clients—the poor, the damaged, the wrong color or background—are easily shoved out of sight, out of mind, offering fodder for our jails and shelters and mental health institutions. Boundary leaders who are drawn to the broken spaces can be caught in the careless crossfire of funding cuts, shifting political priorities, changing mission fashions.

Millicent is an example of the intentional vulnerability of boundary leaders. Leaving her civil service job to respond to

God's call to the ministry, she entered the unguarded world of the boundary zone. Her south Louisiana home church, however, refused to credit God's call of a black woman to the ministry. She moved to Alexandria, where at last a new congregation affirmed her efflorescent spirituality and licensed her to preach. Income supplemented by love offerings from parishioners, without insurance and thereby subject to all the health risks a fiftyish black woman faces, Mildred is highly exposed to boundary zone damage. Nobody wishes her ill, but her problems are her own, not some institution's.

Like Millicent, most boundary leaders are regarded with suspicion by their organization: first, in their allegiance; second, in their commitment. There is, admittedly, justification for that feeling on the part of the employing organization. Indeed, it is usual for anyone working in the boundary zone that his or her first allegiance and first commitment is always to someone more significant than "the boss," always to an ideal or concept more valuable than the bottom line. Boundary leaders, unless they are financially independent, work to earn a living. Many seek, and find, positions that align with their boundary zone ambitions: hospital chaplains, public health workers, social workers, community organizers, missionaries, pastors. Nevertheless, whether their boundary leadership is done as a vocation or as an avocation, as they lean into their communities, they weave relationships that compete for their allegiance with the organization that pays them. Their heart, their loyalty, cannot be confined within structures; their soul, their commitment, cannot be restrained by walls.

All clergy, even small-church clergy, are accountable to someone: elders or deacons or vestry, who often wonder why the pastor is wandering around the community so much. While a small church is a simple organization, it has infinite relationships to tend inside the circle. One way commonly used to judge the success of the pastor's "external" work is whether the interior grows in members and/or income. If the pastor's primary allegiance, goes the reasoning, is to the church, "success" (that is, increase) will be the outcome.

Churches are often (appropriately) accused of such simplistic thinking. But it is the rare organization, sacred or secular, that does not practice similar accounting of its employees' roles in the community. Parish nurses, for example, are usually employed by health systems or large congregations to reach out to community members with health concerns. This commonly translates into, first and foremost, furthering the goals of the corporation or focusing primarily on the needs of the members of the sponsoring large churches, tasks that limit the nurses' ambitions to build community coalitions and initiate caring networks beyond the enclave that may be paying them. Unless the organization is part of a larger system that finds its success through enhancing the vitality of the larger system—and it is a remarkable organization that sees itself in this role—boundary leaders such as parish nurses are constantly forced to explain their role and value under suspicion of having a divided heart.

 # Profile: *Donrico Colden*

The Reverend Donrico Colden knows that telling the truth is more than a simple recitation of facts. The prophetic sharing of truth embraces what can be, what should be, and sometimes even what must be. Each day he faces two realities as the Spiritual Care Coordinator for Pinnacle Health, a system of four hospitals in Harrisburg, Pennsylvania. He must make sure that the spiritual care of each individual is not overlooked in the vast Pinnacle system; and he must include churches, synagogues, and mosques in delivering spiritual care for the thousands of patients.

"I am more or less the conscience of the corporate culture," he says. "It's a prophetic role. It is about lifting up the values and beliefs of persons who come here to be cared for. I remind those who are in positions of power and influence of the value of faith and spirituality in the practice of medicine. I emphasize person-hood in a time when hospitals are so technical in the delivery of services. Our patients are human beings with social and spiritual histories. They come in with all sorts of medical complications, but they also have spiritual needs. I was hired to see to it that those needs are addressed."

The Pinnacle system's concern for patients' spiritual health existed before Colden became Spiritual Care Coordinator in 2000. His task is making sure a busy staff does not forget the "other dimension" of health care. With seven hundred beds and a large hospital staff, Colden is a one-person department with a team of volunteers. "The system hired me to deal with all of this," he says. "I remember the people hiring me said they weren't sure my job would be possible. But I said, 'I can do this.'"

His confidence is the product of his call. As a local pastor, Colden "felt really frustrated trying to transform thinking, or try-ing to get people to begin to be more mission- and community-oriented. We served sandwiches on Saturday at a homeless shelter, but I kept asking, 'What about the other six days of the week?'"

Colden served in several parishes, mostly in the central Pennsylvania area. A Harrisburg native, he was aware of how neighborhoods were deteriorating. "There was a lot of suffering in people's lives." At an early age, he realized that the church had something to say to that suffering.

"When I went to church as a youngster, I really paid attention. So I was getting all of this information and hearing the words of our Lord, and then seeing the suffering in the real world. It left me thinking, 'There is something wrong with this picture.' I wanted to be a minister so I could do it right."

Colden turned to the hospital chaplaincy after an IHP meeting about health disparities and faith community opportunities. "I thought, 'Ah ha! That's it!' I'd never seen the connection so clearly. Public health and faith institutions had to come together to improve the quality of people's health.

"I wasn't comfortable in the pulpit just preaching it," Colden recalls. "I'd end up fighting with my church boards and committees, asking when we were going to get out and do grassroots ministries. I started to dread committee meetings. We were counting our pennies and bemoaning what resources we didn't have. And then we'd hear 'This Is Our Father's World' on Sunday morning. For me, the question became, 'Do we or don't we trust this, will we or won't we do what needs to be done?'"

As a student, Colden had enjoyed biology and the sciences. As he "burned out in the ministry," he says, he turned toward Clinical Pastoral Education (CPE) because "that's where science and theology became wedded. In CPE I began to connect science as part of my call. It helped me get in touch with my unique self. Chaplains were speaking the language that I was speaking, and the CPE association became a community. These people were interested in other disciplines, in the science of health care, in policy issues, and in public policy. They were looking at the systems."

As part of his CPE training, Donrico worked in geriatrics and rehabilitation at a nursing facility. He saw the miracles of medical science in healing patients with broken hips, the need for spiritual strength during months of rehabilitation, and the importance of prayer as part of the process. On an individual level, his call was complete. On a wider scale, however, more needed to be done.

"I had prayed to God to allow me to be in ministries without having to deal with the infrastructures of the church." At Pinnacle, he has felt free to be an advocate for concerns he believes are vital to community health. He recognizes too that as the sole chaplain, he cannot provide the necessary spiritual care to thousands of patients single-handedly. "It really is a matter of collaboration, and providing leadership for true collaborations. One must work with others to accomplish goals and objectives."

Pinnacle Health gives millions of dollars in health care each year to those who cannot pay for it. But through Colden's office, it is encouraging churches to volunteer resources at hand: nurses who can monitor the health of church members; individuals who, with training, can help; lay ministers who can extend spiritual care to neighborhood residents. "We're saying, 'Look at what you've got and put it to use.'"

Colden feels comfortable urging churches to volunteer, because he has done it himself. "This, of course, deals with one's call. What is my call to this ministry? Without a call you grow weary in a hurry and drop out of the race. I hear our Lord saying, 'Count up the cost.' A real grassroots ministry is not about having your name up in lights. We have to have gifts that come along with the call, but without the call, there are not the gifts. The call comes first."

Allegiance and Commitment, Intellect and Action

Like many sprawling urban areas, Atlanta is mostly boundary zone with miles of territory under ambiguous and contested control. It is constantly trying to make sense of itself and its future through a stream of meetings and summits. You can tell from several counties away if the meetings are designed under old-style coalitions of organizational leaders who seek to negotiate the application of their shared power, sometimes wrestling to gain more. Boundary leaders enter into community-scale processes suspected by those in their own organizations as well as those from outside. A few years ago at a meeting in Atlanta focusing on mercy and justice of health care services, I noted that participants—all of us—felt restricted in our freedom to discuss the multilayered and unjust tangle of power lurking beneath the surface of our complaints because many of us were paid by organizations that were part of that power elite.

Academics notice the same nervousness about relationships across the boundaries of their professions, especially by tenure committees. The viewpoint: If the professor is dedicated to advancing *her* or *his* discipline (theology, for instance), why is he or she talking to those folks across campus (in public health, for instance)?

Examples are found even among those in the "objective" scientific disciplines. Although every academic discipline has emerged for a useful intellectual purpose, its survival today often reflects other priorities and processes. Disease specialists compete with one another for political and financial supremacy. A diabetes specialist risks the ire of peers by collaborating too closely with a cardiovascular community initiative. Violence researchers compete with those studying HIV/AIDS or tobacco, who themselves are reluctant to give way to broad-based positive interventions such as "youth development." Community partners are forgiven for noticing that the various diseases are oddly competitive, but any boundary leader funded by one of the categorical disease programs says so only by raising suspicions of their allegiance to one's colleagues.

Public health was once nearly inseparable from the field of social work, especially in its commitment to eliminate poor housing, bad food and water, and unsafe working conditions. But for at least two generations, public health has been dominated by specialists working from an infectious-disease medical model, which focuses on the infectious agent, not the social context. Today public health struggles to find its way back toward comprehensive social and ecological determinants of health—the boundary zone—but existing intellectual and funding patterns make it an uphill walk.

Such conflicts both frustrate and bypass boundary leaders, since their primary allegiance and total commitment is to that which is emerging, not to ideologies or programs trapped in containers of the past. The emergent is often formed from the most vital pieces breaking free from old intellectual and programmatic forms, often as natural mutations or extensions of the field.

Boundary leaders' thinking leaps across the chasms of uncertainty and restraint, of doubt and confusion, making connections that sweep across the front lines of issues and fields. They want a synoptic worldview: all the parts spread out side by side where one can trace the interconnections at a glance. They become good at synthesizing ideas from disparate, fragmented information. They see their roles—and their lives—as a struggle for both social justice and the development of an inner life, for their sense of the sacred includes personal growth, service to others, and social activism. As mapped by Ray and Anderson in *Cultural Creatives*,[3] boundary leadership represents a sort of ragged convergence of five formerly distinct streams:

> Boundary leaders' thinking leaps across the chasms of uncertainty and restraint, of doubt and confusion, making connections that sweep across the front lines of issues and fields.

- the ecology movement (as distinguished from conventional environmentalism)
- feminism
- alternative health care
- self-actualization psychology
- spirituality with a psychological (as opposed to traditional religious) focus.

This is quite a stew of ideas, assumptions, languages, organizational agendas, conceptual leaders, and alliances. Not all boundary leaders are comfortable with the full gamut. But most subscribe to a comparably complex set of tributary allegiances flowing into their own personal transformation and their hopes for community transformation.

A more troubling suspicion regards the intellectual depth of boundary leaders, and again it is an inherent character of those moving in the boundary zones. My own "field" of public health and faith borrows from theology, public health (itself a complex ensemble), medicine, sociology (especially of religion, but not just Christian and not just in the United States), political systems, and leadership (like public health, a complex conceptual mélange). Oh, and you will have noticed a heavy borrowing in this book from the still-forming field of complexity theory. I can argue and do that the nature of our human challenges embedded in disparities, poverty, and ecology give us no other place to go than to the intersection of these fields. But how is it remotely possible for one human in our few allotted decades to achieve anything like competence across such a range?

It is hard even to learn how to pronounce the bigger words in each component field, much less master the intricacies of the field. Each of the fields is far from static. Indeed, each field I name is a multiplicity of journals and subdisciplines with thousands of active scholars digging an intellectual lacework deeper into the soil like the webs of diamond tunnels beneath Kimberly. Boundary leaders cannot avoid complexity—intellectual, theological, programmatic, political, emotional. Unbounded complexity is the very definition of the boundary zone. But we should not be surprised when those with particular depth suggest that we do not master *any* of the components of the complexity.

I once taught a class on poverty at a local arts school. The dean explained that many of the students felt strongly about social issues, but did not know anything about them and hoped that in a semester I could bring them up to speed on the issues, at least poverty. (Fortunately, most of the artists go harmlessly into advertising, where simplistic thinking fits right in.)

Even those with the most impeccable credentials experience suspicion as they move toward the boundary zone. *Dying*

for Growth: Global Inequality and the Health of the Poor was produced by a stunning array of boundary scholars affiliated with
the Institute for Health and Social Justice.[4] It is a work of pas-
sionate scholarship and proves the terms are not antithetical.
As Paul Farmer says in the foreword, "the books of the
Institute are written by scholars—anthropologists, epidemiologists, historians and political economists—but they are
prompted by the concerns of doctors and patients."[5] The
exploration of the new economic world order's effect on the
health of the poor involved 27 case studies and was equipped
with 83 pages of footnotes and a 55-page bibliography.
Required reading within the narrow field of public health and
human rights, the book has been found lacking in depth by
many in positions of power.

Farmer followed with *Pathologies of Power,* with a foreword
by Nobel Prize–winning economist Amartya Sen, who praised
Farmer's failure to "fall for the temptation of a make-believe
exactness."[6] Farmer explains his case-study approach by
describing twenty-four hours of a visit to Chiapas, Mexico:
"The images and events we experienced during these twenty-
four hours—rummaging Mexican soldiers, a martyred teenager
and a martyred bishop, the workshop of well-meaning elites
from the capital, a mental health project involving exhuma-
tion, a cry against neoliberalism—encapsulate as well as anything can the heart of what I hope to write about."[7] A
MacArthur "genius award" recipient, a Harvard physician, and
a Ph.D. anthropologist with decades of experience on the bitter ground of poor people's medicine, Farmer does not fear, but
is never surprised by, the accusation that he is moving beyond
the data, in over his head. No boundary leader engaging disparities in health in the smallest Louisiana village engages any
less complexity, although they do so with little of the professional cover that Farmer commands.

One could argue that anyone who resists the exploration of
complexity is guilty of the same presumption. To imagine that
one could rationally contain the discussion of disparities

within the field of health sciences, much less any one of the categorical programmatic areas, is ludicrous at first glance. But the disparities at least, back onto complexity rather than moving boldly into the contested domain.

The intellectual suspicion is not simply political, although it is easy to see it as such. The charge is legitimate, one that boundary leaders should respond to with personal humility and a willingness to be corrected in any particular. What boundary leaders cannot do is seek the safety of any one of the favored intellectual grottos.

Profile:
Larry James

Life may seem just fine, until one becomes aware that just down the road, just across the tracks, just there at the edge of the safe and settled neighborhood, is another world: a world of need and hurt and hopelessness, of despair and degradation, of loneliness and rage. Most of us turn away; the boundary leader turns toward. For "just fine" is not fine at all.

Once Larry James had seen the boundaries, life changed. James, executive director of Central Dallas (Texas) Ministries, is the son of West Texas cotton farmers who moved to Spokane, Washington, where Larry was born; then to Des Moines, Iowa; then to Richardson, a suburb of Dallas that James likens to the television town of Mayberry. The homes are beautiful, the town pleasing, the schools full of hope for the future. The poor did not live in Richardson.

Church became a mainstay of James's life. "My father and mother were compassionate, great people, and still are," James says. At church and at home, he learned to have a concern for others.

After college and graduate work in theology, James pastored in Shreveport, Louisiana. The church sat on the boundary between an affluent white and a poor black neighborhood. Fresh out of seminary and idealistically aware of Christ's work with those who had been excluded, James preached a gospel of change.

"I like to tell people that I was in Shreveport for two years and 45 minutes, because I had the audacity to bring black kids to church," he says with a laugh. "It didn't sit too well."

He could have ignored the situation. Or worked slowly either to change his congregation or to change himself. But in a true boundary leader, outrage has a way of gathering single-minded energy. Sunday segregation and weekday unconcern were not part of James's agenda. Not surprisingly, his next call was to a congregation where the two worlds met in a single place.

While attending the Baptist seminary in New Orleans, James worked in a church with a weekday ministry to street people; he helped start a day care center. On Sunday the church met one set of needs; during the week, another set of needs. A single church nourishing two communities fed James's imagination.

In 1980 "the church where I grew up called me to be pastor." Whereas the New Orleans church was in a blighted area, Richardson was comfortably affluent and the thousand-member church was one of the "best" in the area. The downside, James knew, was the people of Richardson expected conservative evangelical preaching. The upside was his children would attend excellent schools in a "safe" neighborhood. But James could not forsake the calling he had had in New Orleans.

"The terribly limiting theological perspective of that church, I learned, was a bankrupt way of providing new life. I was on a pathway moving away from that viewpoint. Just beneath the affluence was lots of poverty, lots of disrespect for the poor—abject poverty wasn't far away."

James began trying to move church members to a more "open and ecumenical" stance. He laughs. "I was many a pastor's answer to prayer on how to grow a church, because I ran so many people away from mine! Lots of people left." But "lots who were looking for a spiritual path that made sense" began to replace the deserters.

The congregation planned a two-million-dollar renovation. James thought the money could be put to better use. He recalls: "I had asked them to be patient with me about the building. I said there was no way I could do that, and asked them to pray about it and put the renovation on hold for a while."

Within six months, a developer offered more than $2 million for church land. The congregation sold and moved two miles down the road. The new sanctuary was half the size of the old one but totally multipurpose, with a ministry center that was more conducive to an open ministry.

James started working with Latin American refugees. The church became involved in the Sanctuary movement. "Helping these people led us into an ecumenical posture," James says. "It was an incredibly formative time."

A medical doctor friend of James had patients who were HIV positive. "They are searching for spiritual roots," he told James, "and I don't know where to send them."

Mike, a dental student with full-blown AIDS, was the first to come. "During our first conversation, he shared that he had come over to see if we could develop a relationship that would allow me to preside at his funeral."

Others with AIDS begin to attend. The ministry became so extensive that NBC's *Dateline* reported the work. "It is a crazy thing that when the church decides to do what Jesus did, it is news," James says.

Change, of course, has its inevitable tensions. How does one help individuals within the congregation broaden their boundaries? How can those resistant to change learn that God might be expecting something more of them? How does pastoral ministry work when justice seems to demand so much?

With strong support and direction from the church's board of elders, James balanced a devoted pastoral ministry with a vibrantly prophetic one. When disagreements occurred, there was respect for honest differences of opinion.

Caring for people with HIV/AIDS was just one of the ministries that took root. The church developed a twelve-step program for "everything," established a compassionate ministry for the poor, and found a niche as a cutting-edge church.

In 1994 Central Dallas Ministries (CDM) invited James to become its executive director. The agency had a one-night-a-week clinic, an emergency resource center, a sanctuary for worship, and a lot of potential. James accepted the challenge.

James's management style at CDM is described by the maxim, "If you and I agree on everything, one of us should be fired." In less than a decade, the budget has risen from $200,000 a year to $3.5 million a year. A staff of four grew to a staff of fifty.

Now kids in housing projects receive tutoring, and welfare recipients get job training. Two doctors and a dentist provide health care. Four attorneys handle legal claims. A program helps 18-year-olds coming out of foster care with no place to go. In July 2003 CDM broke ground for a housing project.

Successful as it has been, CDM staffers see much more to accomplish. James believes it will require cooperation and involvement from many more churches—or perhaps church members. "I am aware of the unfortunate limitations of the church," he says. "The thing that drives me crazy about the church is that there is so little connection between faith and public policy. There is no carryover to the shalom of God. So I am constantly barking at the church.

"But out there on the edge are some possibilities. Sometimes you have to get out from under the umbrella of the church and then come back to it and say, 'Hey, would you come help us do this? This is the Macedonian call. This puts legs under your faith.'"

James continues: "I'm a simple-minded guy, but I've discovered two things. First, 90 percent of everything is showing up; second, what's left is not going away. If you just keep showing up, eventually things work out. I love the saying that you don't win the World Series by hitting home runs; you win the World Series with singles. I don't actually think of myself as a boundary leader. I just keep showing up and trying to relate to people."

Strengths of Boundary Leaders

The weaknesses felt by boundary leaders are not "merely" psychological and emotional. There are real vulnerabilities that offer predictable exposure to wounds, disappointments, and legitimate fears. Boundary leaders emerge because the very force of life draws them out and up toward the vital arenas where the future is trying to be born. Boundary leaders are adapted to the boundary zones, which makes their weaknesses only relative to their full character. To understand why boundary leaders are able to thrive personally and exert such hopeful influence on the systems they inhabit, we must look at the pattern of their strengths.

Boundary leadership aligns assets in light of mature faith and relevant science. The sole tools to accomplish the alignment are shared vision and the kind of deep and tenacious commitment the Bible calls "covenant" that leads to sustained purposeful action. The strengths of boundary leaders, often unnoticed even by themselves, are perfectly suited to that work. It is rare for boundary leaders to know their own strengths. Even when they are succeeding at the work in the boundary zone, they are judging themselves by old inside-the-container criteria.

> **Boundary leaders emerge because the very force of life draws them out and up toward the vital arenas where the future is trying to be born.**

Boundary leaders are adapted to the margins, to the spaces on the edges, to the land between. They experience those margins as a gift that enables them to midwife community change. They live amid an unusually broad network of relationships, most of them shallow, but they weave the pastor, the clerk, the scholar, the scientist, the politician, the official—that vast assembly of friends, acquaintances, and personal connections—into a hub of information, emergent vitality, powerful agents for change. They frequently link one part of this complex web of relationships to another in ways that are unpredictably wise. They are resilient. They are imaginative, with the capacity to see patterns of possibility. Perhaps surprisingly, they also have great organizational intelligence, a bit like the rabbit knows the fox or the sergeant knows the general.

In *Common Fire*, the authors describe a cohort of people drawn out from their narrow tribes into what they call the Global Commons, which is "global in scope, diverse in character, and dauntingly complex. A radically interdependent world economy has dissolved old boundaries, loosed waves of migrant labor, triggered smoldering cultural conflicts, and forced profound social and political reorganization at all levels. We are simultaneously fragmented into loose and shifting associations of individuals, interest groups, and tribes, yet drawn more closely into a larger web of life."[8] Boundary leaders appreciate, because they engage, this social boundary zone.

The Gift of Marginality

Common Fire notes that there are two kinds of marginality; one is based on vulnerability, the other reflects distinctive values that place one apart from the center of the culture. This second definition most accurately describes the boundary leader. "The single most important pattern we have found in the lives of people committed to the common good is . . . a call to a *constructive, enlarging engagement with the other.*" This, of course, necessitates not only some sense of identity with those who are "different," but also a willingness—an urgency, perhaps—to cross boundary lines to assist them in their need. Boundary leaders move across the boundaries between tribes because they live on the edge of their own tribe. "Especially when parents, teachers, and others help to interpret the difference in positive ways, marginality may place [a boundary leader] in a position to recognize more easily the stranger next door."[9]

Morality-based marginality results from being part of a family or subgroup whose unique values distinguish them in generally admirable ways from the rest of the tribe. Dr. Fran Wenger is a senior scholar of IHP; before her retirement, she guided our work with academic partners. A Mennonite married to a linguist, Fran exemplifies one gifted with marginality. Although she tells of the tension of finding her way out from the conservative core of Mennonite culture, her life was stamped with the imprint of a religious community that shares a distinctive and "respected heritage" that expects all its members "to practice an uncommon regard for others." Not surprisingly, Fran moves with ease, even delight, across boundaries of tribe, culture, race, class, and academic discipline.

Not too many white Protestant male Americans receive this gift of marginality, but I did by being raised in a part of Baltimore County dominated by Jewish and Catholic families. I am not sure my parents even realized what a minority they were, but I did. I had a sharp sense of my distinctive identity: Methodist (!) and Republican (!). I remember the lonely walk from my high school to stuff envelopes in the campaign office of some hopeless Republican candidate. I once went to a Republican dinner for some soon-to-be-slaughtered nominee; I was astonished to find two hundred people present. Until that moment I had no idea we were such a robust group!

I felt a call to the ministry in junior high school and went to Wake Forest University in the late 1960s expecting to become an Army chaplain. In my freshman year, while in ROTC, I saw my world, torn by the national agony of Vietnam, in a radical new light. In a period of painful months, I found myself forced to turn away from my suburban Republican tribe. I remember assuming that Jesus would have to go too. But Ed Christman, a college chaplain, saved my life-in-the-church by making me read the writings of civil rights leader Martin Luther King and war protester Daniel Berrigan. Their words gave me a new marginality (on the left, not right, margin) that ironically felt the same and thus like home (I became an "interfaith liberal Baptist"). I now see how the early gift of marginality made it possible for me to live so comfortably on a new margin and to move with comfort across many others since.

Boundary leaders, gifted by values of the margins, see boundaries as places where differences thrive, and they like it there. While assuming neither conflict nor confluence, they create channels and bridges of understanding involving race, wealth, gender, profession, academics, age, and faith. One of the boundary leaders I interviewed started young:

> My senior year in high school was the first year that we had integrated, and I ran for student council president on a platform that we needed to get over this anger and get over this racism. As a seventeen-year-old I don't know if I articulated very well, but I tried to demonstrate in reaching out to the black students in the school. [She won.]
>
> I was involved in some of the Vietnam era protests and civil rights work and came face-to-face with people who had some diametrically opposed views, values, and I've been yelled at. Over the course of time I've come to be less tolerant of intolerance but at the same time I've come to some understanding of the possibilities that even people of faith and people of good will can have very strong arguments about things.[10]

Vulnerability-based marginality, experienced by three-fifths of those in the *Common Fire* study, is a "consequence of circumstance, not choice: racial discrimination, sexual orientation, physical disability, intellectual or educational attainment, illness, family pain, poverty—even the isolation of wealth. . . . Although few would wish it on others, most have been able to transform the pain of their marginality into a deepened capacity for compassion and a strength of identity and purpose."[11]

It is critical, of course, that the vulnerability is experienced and interpreted in the context of a family or community that builds resilience, compassion, empathy, and hope. The Fifth Ward of Houston is like many other vulnerable neighborhoods in urban America; its health data are dismal and its poverty visible for blocks. But unlike most, it has produced several generations of national, indeed *transnational*, leaders, such as Mickey Leeland and Barbara Jordan, who moved from the ward with a global empathy and passion for justice that remained on a slow boil for their whole lives. They were just as vulnerable as other kids raised in and near poverty, surrounded by a hostile and demeaning white culture. But their marginality, tempered in the culture of a community that never gave up on justice, turned into a gift that benefited many beyond their tribe. "The central gift of marginality is its power to promote both empathy with the other and a critical perspective on one's own tribe. . . . When one stands at the margins, astride the boundary between tribes, one stands also at the center of a larger and more adequate whole."[12]

Frequently boundary leaders, marginalized by their values, find themselves among the vulnerable marginalized too. Millicent, who demonstrated her power to bless at the beginning of the chapter, understood the need for blessing because of her own vulnerability. After a lifetime in a secure civil service job, she is now among the uninsured because of her call to the boundaries. The flow of midcareer women, many leaving more secure financial positions to follow a summons of spirit similar to Millicent's, crosses a number of theological and guild boundaries. If they find a church at all, many find themselves in small (marginal) congregations with few resources, little respect from their denomination, curiosity from their communities, bouncing along on the bottom ranges of the middle class. Add the existential exposure of all the predictable weaknesses of boundary leaders and they may find it hard to hear marginality as any kind of gift. Their other strengths, often unnamed or unappreciated, are the source of their resilience. It is also the key to their *relevance*—to the emergence of that for which they hope.

Those with the gifts of marginality are hard to surprise. Their hopes protect them from cynicism, but their marginality protects them from naïveté. Rather than moving into the future amazed at the capacity of systems for arrogance, accident, collateral damage, and thoughtlessness, boundary leaders know what to expect. This has defensive implications: they are hard to sneak up on, harder to sabotage, not quite so easy to deflect and distract with typical organizational strategies. On the other hand, boundary leaders are able to see the cracks in the system's own cynicism where the remnants of justice and mercy live. Dr. King quoted with integrity the words of religious spirituals *and* the founding documents of the United States, all of which called for justice. He knew the system that had counted men like him as three-fifths of a person. He also saw the crack in the system's own logic that could not deny the emergence of a freedom embedded in democracy. Those on the margins are more likely to see the system in its wholeness, including the parts kept from the view of the privileged.

How many middle-class Americans have the faintest (i.e., not seen on TV) idea of how the criminal justice system works? How many have the slightest clue of the cruel carelessness of a court system that depends on specialized representation far beyond the reach of those below middle class? For that matter, how many upper- and middle-class urbanites know where their food comes from: who plants it, who picks it? How many know the fate of those in other countries who now supply many of our winter vegetables and much of our beef? How many know the salaries, insurance protections, and wage stability of those who flip burgers at fast-food restaurants or clean toilets in motel rooms?

Those gifted with marginality see the system whole, understand how its different facets relate to one another, and thus have some possibility of seeing where it might turn in new ways.

At one of our institutes, a team from North Carolina worked to develop a plan for reversing the vast diabetes disparity

among the Cherokee people. In one exercise, they were asked
to draw a map of the system that created and perpetuates the
problem. Most do this by going back ten or twelve years. The
Cherokee team, under the leadership of a full-blooded
Cherokee woman named Patty, started its map in the 1700s
when their people lost their land, moved on to the "trail of
tears," the forced pilgrimage from North Carolina to
Oklahoma, and cycled into a complex but coherent system of
denial and humiliation often justified by the religious language of most of the others in the room.

Most diabetes specialists see the disease precursors as lack
of exercise and lousy diet. Patty's team, seeing the system
whole, included a broad range of efforts to help the Cherokee
people reclaim their cultural memory. A full appreciation of
the past opens the possibility of seriously working on the
future.

Broad Relationships

Malcolm Gladwell, in *Tipping Point*, reports on a simple sur-
vey he developed to determine if some people knew more people than most of us do.[13] After composing a list of 250
surnames taken at random from the Manhattan phone book,
he asked about 400 people how many of their acquaintances
had those surnames. Some two dozen scored under 20, but
eight had over 90 and four more than 100. Gladwell calls the
high scorers "connectors" because their disproportionate number of relationships makes them hubs of broad networks linking many people with more average numbers of acquaintances.

Boundary leaders frequently describe themselves as having
that kind of extraordinary range of relationships. Even those
who are far from gregarious live on the margins of their
parochial networks; their values draw them into diverse and
wide relationships; their empathy for others draws them
toward others. While intimate friendships are important for
personal survival at the boundaries, a broad network of relationships enhances the boundary leader's potential for success

in efforts to effect systems-level changes. Being easy to find, being comfortable in multiple work zones, being web-centered, being multilingual and/or multicultural—all these give boundary leaders an ability to hurdle barriers that send others to the cinders with skinned knees and sad hearts.

Albert-László Barabási, writing in *Linked* (a book intriguingly subtitled *How Everything Is Connected to Everything Else and What It Means for Business, Science and Everyday Life*), explores the science of networks—relationships that function in seemingly similar ways in many different fields, including the Internet, genetics, marketing, and, of course, human social life. Boundary leaders emerge from and then extend toward networks of relationships that cross the lines otherwise dividing communities into discrete organizations and tribes. The relationships are not random or a simply *designed* hierarchy. Boundary leaders are social hubs with a disproportionate number of human links across which information and influence flow back and forth.

This interconnectedness of the boundary leader rests on a foundation of interpersonal skills, both formal and informal. At their best, the electronic technologies simply allow for the transparency experienced in having, in knowing, and in being known. The vast bulk of communication work involved in aligning community systems is informal; it is what happens over coffee, not a speaker's lectern. An experienced boundary leader in rural South Carolina describes a typical experience:

> My wife and I were going out to dinner downtown last night in Beaufort and happened to run into someone we both knew, who goes to our church, and it just happened we'd been talking about this community development project that we've got going on in a very impoverished area of our community, and we're trying to set up a business incubator out there. The person we ran into just happens to be the Small Business Development person attached to a university branch so we were able to very briefly buttonhole him and say we want to get

together and have a meeting about this project we have going on in this area. Would he be available? Can we sit down and talk? And he expressed real interest in it, so we're going to be able to set that up and bring to bear the university resources on that project. That's what John Wesley called "convenient grace," those things that fall into place, almost a serendipitous matter, but appear to fall in place for a purpose.

If you are trying to maintain the status quo, you need to carefully manage relationships so that they do not disrupt the design. But if the system itself is producing disease and injury as a by-product of its workings *and*—a big "and"—you want to change it, you need webs of relationships that flow outside existing patterns. You need boundary leaders to create relationships that, while not predictable, give priority to those who suffer and those who hope.

A few years ago, a sociology study stumbled on the practical value of "weak" relationships in finding a new job. Twice as many people, the study discovered, found jobs through somewhat distant friends than among close friends. Close friends' networks overlapped, so only a limited number of job possibilities were likely. But a much larger range of opportunity opened up when job seekers extended their networks to include "weaker" connections.

To see how the opportunity of "weak connections" applies to the work of boundary leaders, one need only walk in the door of the Central Dallas Ministries and ask for something, anything. A few months ago I stopped by, and Larry James met me at the door. Walking alongside Larry is to be near a hub of an extraordinary number of relatively "weak ties." Before we made it to the first stairwell, we met a man and young boy; Larry greeted them by name. The African American man, who had brought his son to the clinic, told Larry he had just been laid off. Larry hardly paused; he knew someone who was hiring, a job with benefits and a training program to upgrade computer skills. And we're off. . . . Larry skipped lunch because he was meeting a group of bankers and lawyers to put together a deal for CDM to start a multi-unit housing complex that would bring together the clinic, job training, and multieconomic-level housing.

So his day goes: linking, weaving, connecting, listening, over and across boundaries. In the process his connections create paths that others cross too. Larry is easy to find because his values are well known; he works at the center of great need and community response. So both the links he initiates and those that find him are biased toward people involved in justice and mercy issues. Sometimes the fruit is as simple as a job with benefits; other times it is as unexpected as Dallas bankers investing in a complex interracial, multiclass real estate proposal. But his broad network of relationships, multiplied by other boundary leaders with their own networks, creates an environment in which one can sense the possibility of something truly new, resilient, hopeful emerging in the broken spaces of central Dallas.

Boundary leaders build broad networks of relationships because they have multiple comfort zones. Living on the margins of their own core culture creates the capacity for comfort in multiple settings and among many different people. Larry James moves comfortably from the streets of central Dallas to the country clubs in the suburbs. He may be uncomfortable with the fact that he is comfortable near the surreal green of the golf links, but he actually moves with ease amid the wealthy and the weak. He raises funds for CDM, but also connects at a much deeper level than is necessary for that. He is able to see the full humanity of powerful business people. He pastored for twenty-five years and recognizes spiritual hunger from across a stadium. "I find it easy to not give up on someone who has lost a job and is the wrong color to find another one. My more common sin is to give up on people who know nothing of the man or woman on the streets. I believe more and more in less and less. I know Jesus doesn't give up. That's about it and that ends up taking me some places I would never go to otherwise."

Resiliency

Sometimes it is not pretty or painless; indeed, sometimes the life they lead is pretty painful, but boundary leaders are resilient because they have high tolerance for ambiguity and excellent survival skills. Their optimistic uncertainty about this or that outcome, that or this alternative, is grounded in the absolute certainty that they are on the right track to reach vital community goals—they are, in fact, doing the right thing—and that they are the right person to do it.

Although boundary leaders may experience the boundary zone as a place of brokenness and contested authority, they are not defeated by either the powerful interests that create the pain or by the divisions that threaten to obstruct progress and detour success. Even without looking too deeply into how violence and domination are attracted to broken spaces, it is easy to see how boundary leaders are easily wounded. Their lives are filled with more than the usual relationships among people experiencing brokenness and prone to violence. It is a cohort designed for unpredictability. Boundary leaders are not slick, sliding easily around and across unpleasantness. Boundary leaders are "sticky" in their relationships, as Web-site designers speak of some sites as being "sticky" when people tend to pause and engage.

A few decades of boundary life necessitates personal resilience: if you cannot bounce back, you cannot make it in the boundary zone. More importantly, at least from the perspective of the systems under attack, boundary leaders add resilience to community processes. They expect uncertainty and are not frightened by it. They do not expect it to go away, so they do not fear a long and uncertain path walked with an uncertain and unlikely group of people. They expect to be wounded, because they have been before; but they also expect the wounds not to be fatal to themselves or to the hopes that draw them forward. Thus they are not surprised when a project experiences trouble or even breaks into pieces. They have seen disarray before and recognize it as a step toward order.

Boundary leaders' high tolerance for ambiguity contradicts the highly stable, hierarchical structure of most organizations where corporate memory brings stability, even in infrequent circumstances. Organizational people have seen it all before; they know how power works in the system and the range of possibilities. The boundary zones, however, require an opposite outlook, because events are unscripted, people unpredictable, outcomes uncertain—here situations *are* ambiguous and insecure. Nobody has stood exactly on this spot before: the possibilities implicit in the newly emergent patterns, the partners, the relevance and capacities of the powers, the time frame are all unknown and unknowable. This uncertainty is known by veterans of the boundary zones. This is their home and where they find their peace. Boundary leaders appreciate ambiguity, not just as something to be endured, but as the experiment in which hope bubbles out of the test tube. Boundary leaders can see in dark places because they do not fear the night.

Romie Lilly, whom we met back in chapter 2, is the kind of boundary leader powerful interests tend to overlook. Associate pastor in a small Baptist church in a backwater Los Angeles neighborhood, Romie is the hub of an extraordinary range of people—addicts of many kinds of power, chemical, political, and violent. For years his health has been fragile, even disabling. He walks slowly with a cane. He may be the only person in L. A. County who cannot drive, which makes his constant motion hard to understand. In a city filled with flash and disaster, Romie survives. His resilience gives him a rich memory of strategies, people, processes, resources—ways to make it through. More sophisticated than any "artificial intelligence," Romie's *integral* intelligence makes survival likely, almost dependable, if never predictable, for either himself or his projects.

Boundary leaders need survival skills. They are not so much clever as tenacious, not so much quick as tough. If they were boxers, they would be able to take a punch. Because they have hopes that many do not share, they can take a defeat and turn the other cheek. The authors of *Common Fire* note that many of those working in the "commons" change jobs and many other things while keeping their core hope alive. "Rather than relinquish the commitment, people are more likely to question the form of their work or particular strategy."[14]

Personal wounds hurt; sometimes they produce lingering fear, even shame, that repels one from uncertain situations and new relationships. But no group, congregation, coalition, or company is qualified to engage complex community dynamics if it does not have members who have been wounded. When groups ask me to help them discern their strategy for community engagement, I often begin by asking them to complete a "qualifications for ministry scan" (see page 96). Members of the group initial each of the boxes for which they are "qualified." Most of the qualities would be considered wounds—just the kind of thing you would not want others to know, exactly the opposite of what most consider qualifications for personal success. You would not want your banker or mother-in-law to see a fully completed scan. But how could a church have an intelligent hope for the homeless, if none of its members had ever been homeless, or cold, or hungry, or jobless; if none had ever visited a thrift store to buy shoes for a child, or received government assistance, or worked a minimum-wage, no-benefits job? The resilience of a group rests partly on its corporate compassion based on the cumulative experiences of the whole. Indeed, on a personal basis, this is part of how the wound heals. It becomes a corporate asset as it is brought into the circle of grace and made part of the healing of the larger community.

"Resilience would be a kind of pitifully slow learning, if it was not fed by a deep reservoir of hope." King encouraged many of us to believe that history tended toward justice, if slowly."[15] King died young, but his dream is still young and, yes, resilient. King's own capacity to suffer, to work amid profound ambiguity, to speak with integrity and hope at the same time built resilience into the movement to which he gave his life.

Figure 4

Qualifications for Ministry Scan
1. Find someone in the group who has experienced each of the following and get their initial in the block.
2. Note that many of these are personally painful, but are *community* qualifications for ministry.

Lost a job	Seen a $500 bill (American currency)	Started a business	Changed jobs on purpose	Had a child fail, been held back in school	Wrote a magazine article
Preached a sermon sort of about justice	Birthed a child	Played basketball outdoors	Saw your child graduate from high school	Speaks Spanish	Buried a parent
Sang a solo in public	Gotten laughed at in public	Lost an election for public office	Held office in a civic organization	Run a day care center of some sort	Run more than 5 miles (at one time)
Been paid to play a sport	Prayed in a public gathering	Stayed one night in the home of another race	Prayed with a Muslim in a mosque	Knows a Buddhist by first name	Been arrested for civic disobedience
Spent more than one night in jail	Been assaulted or "mugged"	Spent more than one night in a hospital	Lived more than one month without health insurance	Seen a rat in a house	Paid back taxes for a mistake
Lived in this city for 10 years	Buried a child	Lived in five cities for one year	Worked in a welfare office	Paid property tax in the city	Speaks French
Spent more than two days and nights hungry	Lost physical capacity due to car accident	Served in armed forces in combat	Knows a political prisoner	Voted in the last five local elections	Milked a cow
Washed dishes for money	Started a non-profit organization	Knew a person who committed suicide	Delivered a meal to a homebound person	Been present at a non-family member's death	Had cancer
Been overweight	Participated in a racist action of some kind	Been alone in a foreign country	Been alone in nature for 24 hours	Blended a family from two marriages	Been a member of a non-Christian faith group
Voted Republican (on purpose)	Received a government scholarship	Sailed a boat out of sight of land (and back)	Smokes	Children attending another faith	Been in counseling
Applied for government assistance	Lost 50 pounds (on purpose)	Volunteered in church missions project	Recovering from alcohol dependency	Led a 12-step group	Coached a youth sports team
Performed a role on stage	Received financial help from a church	Written a song performed in public	Had a book or article or song rejected	Cried outside the home	More than one year without a church home
More than 10 years without a church home	Got government funding for a project	Driven a bus	Performed an operation on somebody	Quit smoking	Struck another person in anger
Been shot at	Home burglarized	Voted Democrat (on purpose)	Lost a home due to bankruptcy	Been cold more than 48 hours in a row	Has HIV or a family member who does

Imagination

Boundary leaders have strength of imagination, a subtle capacity to see what could be. They have the capacity to learn and discern. This gives them a wide range of images of hope. They imagine using all four frames: structure, power, human capacity, and meaning. Ironically, their store of unfulfilled dreams feeds imagination.

Inside an organization, imagination is almost something to apologize for: "he is very imaginative" or, worse, "she imagines too much" is a way of saying "do not let the imaginative near power." Inside a power structure imagination is mostly about how-what-already-is-can-remain-so. In the boundary zone, imagination is what makes it possible for webs of transformation to emerge out of chaos. Imagination is the magnet around which relationships form in ways that resonate and then reinforce the images of hope before that hope is visible.

Some think that imagination is a solitary, eyes-shut experience of conjuring fantastic possibilities out of nothing. On the contrary, it is a social, eyes-wide-open experience of seeing reality—the whole of systems and networks, the interconnections and the disjointedness. What *might* be is embedded in what is, however painful it might seem to be. Wendell Berry describes the profound failure of economic imagination: "Most of us cannot imagine the wheat beyond the bread, or the farmer beyond the wheat, or the farm beyond the farmer, or the history beyond the farm. Most people cannot imagine the forest and the forest economy that produced their houses and furniture and paper; or the landscapes, the streams, and the weather that fill their pitchers and bathtubs and swimming pools with water. Most people appear to assume that when they have paid their money for these things they have entirely met their obligations."[16]

Berry's essay, like many of his, reflects a social process of thinking deeply. He continues, "Even now, after centuries of reductionist propaganda, the world is still intricate and vast, as dark as it is light, a place of mystery, where we cannot do one thing without doing many things, or put two things together without putting many things together. Water quality, for example, cannot be improved without improving farming and forestry, but farming and forestry cannot be improved without improving the education of consumers—and so on."[17]

Boundary leaders, because they live in webs of transformative relationships, think and envision at the scale of the system. This is not a personal virtue, something they "have." It is a capacity they experience, nurture, sustain, encourage—all in the webs of relationship of which transformation is the fruit. The images of hope are not something they give to their friends, like some corporate "visionary's" announcement to stockholders. Boundary leaders act as midwives to the imagination, listening, reflecting, and looking carefully for patterns and people and power.

At any given time, the images that matter most may deal with structure, power, human capacity, or meaning. Imagination in any of these categories can illuminate possibilities of action: for next Monday, as well as for a decade away. Boundary leaders boil a rich stew of experiences, people, relationships, and organizational encounters that makes imagination as much a work of memory as it is of anticipation. For them, imagination is often the task of rearranging the past so that the puzzle might piece together the future.

It is no small feat to see strengths where most seek weakness, to see vitality where most see pathology. In my earlier book, *Deeply Woven Roots*, I laid out a framework of eight congregational strengths that are relevant to community health and wholeness. These are somewhat annoying to people trained to *fix* congregations' weaknesses. The strengths enable church members to see their congregation as a place of possibilities that emerge from the alignment of its social strengths with the needs and *opportunities* in its neighborhood environment. Expecting strengths makes it possible to see them, and through them new images of how those strengths are part of God's intentions for wholeness.

Dr. Bradley Gray, one of the faculty of our Institute for Public Health and Faith Collaborations, helps arouse the imaginations of many boundary leaders. He does not give them images, but a set of mirrors in which they can bring themselves into focus. One of the most powerful times in our institute is when he guides team members through a leadership inventory analysis. This is a complex and private process that develops a matrix of leadership tendencies that are unique to each person. But in the context of the team, such self-knowledge feeds a powerful sense of group strength. The vision of a powerful, sustainable *team* grows from the transparency of the members. The greater the transparency, the clearer the image of what is possible. Boundary leaders, often painfully connected to a wide range of humans and organizations in the boundary zone, have the strength of imagination that is hugely relevant to the hopes for systems change.

The image of boundary zones is subversive to people who prefer their perimeters well defined. They often foster a kind of *dis*imagination that disables the future by intentionally walling it within the tribe, discipline, or language of the present. *Dis*imagination moves defensively against boundary zone emergence by promoting the partial as if it was the whole. This is the fantasy of empire, theocracy, and, ironically, neoliberal globalism because it simplifies human relationship down to economic exchange. Boundary leaders' imagination always sails across those simplifications, powered by the webs of relationship that make anything less than whole-system transformation ring false.

We are often apologetic for our unfulfilled dreams. What are thought useful are the fulfilled dreams that give evidence of our credibility, dependability, and predictability. Organizations count all three as currency. Boundary leaders, living and working in webs of relationship, often have trouble claiming as their own possession the fruits of a complex process. What they have in abundance—hopes, dreams, visions—is counted as mere inspirational fodder.

In the boundary zones, nothing matters more than vital images of what to hope for. The whole process is about emergence toward a wholeness none of us can yet see. We literally see only in pieces in the murk. Nothing matters more than those glimpses of what is possible, even if it is out of reach today. Boundary leaders have many unfulfilled hopes. Better, they imagine what has not yet found its place, its context. My daughter Kathryn enjoys the task of finding a place for a thousand tiny pieces of a large picture puzzle. Any one of those pieces is such a fragment of the whole that it literally makes no sense; together they become a castle sparkling in the sunlight, a snow-covered mountain vista.

> **In the boundary zones, nothing matters more than vital images of what to hope for.**

Many of our hopes are puzzle pieces too. As I write this sentence the warm evening sun moves toward the horizon. I know more than I like about how threatened is the forest that lies between my keyboard and where the sun will set. I have only scraps of hope that have no coherence; the threat to this lush and lovely environment is at the systems level, my hopes are merely personal: an organic garden here, memberships to environmental organizations there . . . the list peters out near despair.

But I do not despair because I am part of webs of transformation that lend me images of hope when my own seem gray and ill defined. To the extent that I am a boundary leader at all, I rest on the strength of the imaginations of the web; I find it is strong enough to lean on.

Profile:
Rabbi Bob Kaplan

Because he is a listener, Rabbi Bob Kaplan is a learner. "I listen to people," he says. "And I am a community organizer with a spiritual imperative. I ground people in the holy, allowing them to see that there is something more going on than they might realize. When we really listen, we can see what is going on around us not just superficially, but in a way that allows for deep change to happen."

Kaplan, who works with the Jewish Community Relations Council of New York's Center for Community and Coalition Building, is rarely in his office. He travels the metro area constantly "trying to put together various resources so things can happen," whether the issue involved is a community program for youngsters or a plan to prevent a SARS outbreak. Two hours after the World Trade Centers fell, Kaplan received a call from the Arab American Family Support Center, with whom he had developed a strong relationship over the previous ten years. They asked him how their members might best respond to the situation.

His call to ministry is still a bit of surprise. Kaplan drifted away from the faith of his childhood, learned the art of Eastern meditation, and lived in a spiritual community. But "in my late twenties I found a rabbi who spoke my language and accepted the commandments as a way of life."

His background has made Kaplan more willing and able to go into new situations and be more understanding. "I love the teaching and the learning. Anytime I can share with new people, it is simply incredible."

He recently traveled to Northern Ireland to teach principles of community organizing to the Protestants and Catholics. He listened carefully not only to what participants said, but also to how they said it, gathering their perceptions of the crisis to see if a deeper vision of common ground might reframe the violence and the injustice.

"When I walk into situations, I am not preaching a religious path," Kaplan says. "I'm just talking about how people should react with each other, and how to understand the needs and desires of other people and other groups.

"When I'm working with new immigrants, for example, the goal is to open them up to what America is all about," he says. "Here I am, an identifiable Jew, and I've become a trusted friend with the Palestinian and Arab American communities because I speak to issues that define us all.

"Dr. King had a vision that deeply affected my life. He said that people with vision can uplift other people around them by helping them see their intrinsic worth. Once that happens, we can all do things we never thought were possible."

Access to health care was the original mission of the Center for Community and Coalition Building. Although health care continues to be a primary emphasis, its mission now includes community organizing. In Far Rockaway, near Kennedy International Airport, Kaplan is working with the faith leaders in the Coalition for Far Rockaway. "We're becoming partners with them on issues like self-esteem," he explains. "We hope to develop a center for literacy, and to break the cycle of violence as it relates to women. We've also started working with immigrant women."

Kaplan also works hard to "maintain tight relationships with the powers that be." "We don't run from those kinds of relationships," he says. "If we are to effect change, we must be in the power structure. If we're outside, it doesn't work."

For him, the sustaining vision is the work of the holy. "What matters is the whole vision of how we interface with God's kingdom," Kaplan says. "Judaism teaches us to look at how God interfaces with the world. When we do, we are given a set of guideposts that show us how to act with the world. God freed the Jews from Egypt; so we must help people when they are suffering. God made sure the people had food in the desert, so we are obligated to feed the hungry. God healed people, so we are obligated to do the same thing.

"All of these lessons are implied when we read the story of God's interface with the world and with humankind. There is no discrimination in any of this. *Tikkun Olam* in Hebrew means 'fixing the world.' God gives us individual pieces of the world to fix, and we're obligated to do that. It's not just our up-and-down relationship with God, but a view of the world that includes our relationship with each other."

Organizational Intelligence

Thinking of themselves on the margins of the organized world, boundary leaders are often surprised to hear they have the strength of organizational intelligence. They live in a world nearly full of organizations, and it is not a pretty picture. Living on the margins, boundary leaders—even, perhaps especially, those working inside large-scale organizations—see that most organizations are not solid and coherent. Their internal contradictions make them far from unified; their leaderships' multiple agendas bring doubts to their best ideas. Most importantly, organizations are filled with people who have a multitude of relationships to each other and to "the organization," as well as highly unpredictable understandings of their own capacities, roles, and missions.

The boundary zone intelligence, which sees things as ambiguous, fluid, emergent, and contested, turns out to be a pretty good way to see organizations too. Organizations are a bit like *semi*permeable boundary zones. Boundary leaders, comfortable with complexity and ambiguity, have a good idea how organizations function and how they do not; what they can do and what they cannot. While this does not equip them to "manage" an organization, it does make it possible for them to dance with it.

Emma Smith is married to Fred Smith, who taught me so much about disparities. Emma co-pastors their tiny church in Ambridge, Pennsylvania, doing most of the nitty gritty boundary work on those tough streets. Emma once explained to me that they were building a church with addicts, whores, and children who have been raised by wolves. It is more complex than that: it includes a former CEO working off a massive bank fraud conviction, repentant corporate executives, a growing gaggle of youth and young couples who sense the possibility of integrity. On principle, they do nothing by themselves: the summer program is conducted jointly with the Episcopal church; a dozen community programs share space with a clutter of government and university programs. Their building is a former Catholic diocese headquarters, complete with school, convent, and gym, that a Presbyterian church from the next town helped purchase. All this does not happen by magic. The Smiths' organizational intelligence is far from ordinary: it is classic boundary leader. Not only do they know how to dance with the powers; they manage to get the powers to dance with one another.

Boundary leaders have the skills needed to dance with the powers. They know how to write grants and work networks, balance the books, and turn off the lights. Or they know how to draw people who know how to do those things into the creative web. But they are not rigidly dancing the two-step like beginners at their first prom; watching Fred and Emma (and all boundary leaders) dance reminds me of the grace and poise and swirling twirling light-as-air movements of Ginger Rogers and Fred Astaire. Their steps are guided by music others inside the old dead walls cannot hear.

 ## Profile:
Fatima Shama

It has been a circuitous career path for Fatima Shama, but at last, the native New Yorker thinks, she has found her calling. Shama directs the Greater Southern Brooklyn Health Coalition, an agency that works with more than a hundred member organizations as diverse as the Church Avenue

Merchants Block Association, Coney Island Hospital, the Jewish Community Council of Flatbush, and Maimonides Medical Center. In a variety of ways, they are all working to overcome health disparities in what would be the United States' fourth largest city, if it were not one of the boroughs of New York City.

Shama quickly points out, "My training is not in health." But health seems, at least for now, where she finds fulfillment and fruitfulness.

With an Arab father and Brazilian mother, Shama speaks English, Arabic, Portuguese, French, and Spanish. Planning to be an obstetrician, she attended a high school designed to prepare students for a career in medicine. But in college she encountered the rough waters of organic chemistry, which, she says, "had the power to change a lot of things." An internship at UNICEF, working on maternal and child health, convinced her to seek a master's degree in public health. The next summer she interned with a community-based organization that focused on immigrant health.

In meetings her outspoken views led friends to suggest she attend law school. "It might be an effective way for you to do what you want to do," they told her. "I thought that was funny and told my parents what people had said. They thought it would be great. After a few years of working, I went to law school at Temple University."

In law school, however, she found it difficult to reconcile a secure career in corporate law with her concerns of conscience and justice. Eventually a professor said to her, "You have to realize you are going into a field that is more corporate than you are."

She left law school and worked for the United Nations in its attempts to secure human rights and provide for public health. Next she joined a group working internationally to affect the lives of women in Africa. That was followed by a job in economic development, helping women make the transition from welfare to work.

"Then September 11 happened." Thoughts of career choice suddenly seemed secondary to primary convictions. "September 11 changed my life drastically as a New Yorker, an American, and a

Muslim," Shama says. "I felt we were plagued by this horrible man's actions. So I started volunteering my time to share what it is to be Muslim. I spent about five months going into high schools and grammar schools. It became a chance for me to correct all of the misconceptions. I wasn't what they expected. It was deeply moving to me because I experienced the good nature of people. People welcomed us into their spaces. It became very evident that people wanted to know who Muslims were.

"At the same time, I'd be in the gym or on the subway and I'd overhear someone saying, 'Why don't they go back where they came from?' I'd realize, they're talking about me. This *is* my home."

Although Shama found her volunteer work rewarding, she still needed a career that would take her vision of what could be done and harness it in a meaningful way. She applied for a job at New York University, but during the interview stage, she met Rabbi Bob Kaplan, who serves as a board member at the Greater Southern Brooklyn Health Coalition (see above, page 101).

Kaplan offered her a job working not with an institution but with many different groups, each focused on justice-related issues. Shama reflected, "I knew it would be a steep learning curve, but they knew it too. So I went with my gut."

One of her first tasks was to write a grant proposal due by Friday.

"Can you do that?" they asked.

"I said, 'I sure can try.'"

Shama's proposal secured the grant. "It was a first victory. I've been here now for a year and a half. I am blessed because I have a group of people who are so supportive. I'll say, 'We have this much money in the bank,' and they'll call and say, 'Don't worry, we'll figure it out.' I am learning so much from them. They put the ball in my court, and ask, 'If we were to do this, how would we do it?' I throw out an idea, and they say, 'Go for it.'"

The coalition is currently "going for" improved health care for immigrants. "Our lobbying helped the city and state recognize some serious issues. The state passed the Child Health Insurance program for all children," Shama says. "We were the energy behind that. It gave us a name. New York City knows we're the group in Brooklyn that deals with health issues.

"A coalition of city health people attends our meetings. We try to really make sure that all the voices are represented and heard, especially the voices of the small community-based organizations, people of many religious, ethnic, and geographic backgrounds."

In southern Brooklyn, heart disease is a major killer. With proper care, it can often be prevented or healed. She envisions walk-to-school campaigns to help young people learn the value of exercise. A school might hold a health fair. A group of Russian immigrants might receive a grant for yoga instruction or tai chi. Each of the hundred organizations that make up the Greater Southern Brooklyn Health Coalition can, in some way, help its members become heart-healthy.

"A property law professor said I'm always fighting for the person who has never had a voice. He said, 'You think that's your responsibility.' I do feel that way, and have thought that way my entire life. I don't know where it comes from, but it is really important that everyone gets a fair chance," Shama says. "And you don't level the playing field by saying you're going to do it, but by hearing people out, and then taking the necessary steps. Those voices may not seem important, even to the speakers, but they are."

Her vision of equality reflects her faith. "A belief in the one God, the author of all creation, who does not exclude and who is merciful and compassionate, is central to Islam."

Working with diverse people, she finds, "is the most rewarding part of my faith. I'm always disappointed when I sense that people are looking at color or social class or education and allowing those differences to divide us. So, in a way, overcoming this attitude of exclusiveness is what I am supposed to do. I happen to be more fortunate than the next, but I know this is not my doing, but God's."

4

Webs of Transformation

A World of Webs

None of us there that day will again turn the page of the calendar from March to April without thinking of her, the child named April. From across the country we had gathered to catch a vision of what our communities could become and how we might make those visions real. Curtis, an epidemiologist from Milwaukee, told us in one word why he went to work: "April."

April was a fourteen-year-old who first came to Curtis's attention as a "case" of syphilis; she later died from AIDS. Hers is not the only name of cruel and chaotic suffering, hers not the only face even in her own neighborhood in her own section of her own city. During the course of our time together, April's name joined that of Jim (in a Montana jail with his family living in a car), Betty (a mentally ill woman on the streets of Baltimore), and many others—the real and honest faces of why we all come to work. I do not know the name of Petros's member that I mentioned in chapter 1. When I tell the story, I often call her Judy, which is the name of my sister. A hospital chaplain, hearing the names, called out "Legion"—

a biblical reference for the many demons Jesus exorcised in the New Testament story—reminding us that each of our sharply remembered faces represents hundreds, thousands, millions we do not and never will know. But to whom we are connected.

Their personal and particular and unique names—their names of Legion—burned into our minds, and in their burning light helped us see the reality of our communities, our cities, our states and regions, our country. Our one linked and shattered world.

April's light disclosed suffering, but also hope. By remembering her clearly enough to reconstruct her spiral down, the Milwaukee leaders found it possible to visualize a constellation of relationships among leaders that could have prevented April's lament. They could see different ways of being together as parents, members of faith groups, leaders of organizations, and builders of communities—to imagine a whole new way of weaving community.

But how will these relationships come to be? What would such relationships look like? For hope once born dies in frustration if it is not nurtured in relationships that wrap it as loam does a seed, enabling it to grow from its warm womb-darkness toward the light. What is needed is a web of transformation.

An acorn has the whole tree within it, every possibility of the full and complex future tree. But it is only a possibility—a seed untransformed, a life unrealized—without the relationships of soil and rain and sun.

What, then, is the nature of the relationships in which transformation can occur? What causes a relationship to sprout and thrive and grow and live on, and, eventually, to replicate itself?

Boundary zones both demand and make possible a social architecture in which new relationships are possible, sustainable, and even powerful. This relational architecture is born of the complex, multilayered, persistent constellation of suffering and hope that is the reality of the boundary zone. Any living thing, if it survives more than one generation, adapts to different ecologies by developing social architectures in which they can live and thrive. So do boundary leaders.

Boundary zones are the ecology in which we find life; the structure in which we are sustained and even thrive in that living is a "web of transformation."

Boundary leaders are always found in webs of transformation: always sustained by those webs, always drawn toward others in those webs. The hope of boundary leaders grows in webs of relationships in which transformation becomes possible. This is where boundary leaders emerge, find their way, do their work, and are sustained over time.

Sometimes webs are a surprise, a serendipitous relationship that sprouts at the point of common work. But once you know what to look for, you can intentionally nurture webs. Webs are alive and must be treated with the respect and reverence living things demand. Webs can be born, but cannot live unless tilled and tended, fertilized and fed. The largest part of the work of boundary leadership is helping webs come to life, find their vital possibility, and grow. Boundary leadership is possible as an intentional practice that can be done well precisely because webs of transformation have pattern and logic, as well as passion and purpose.

In 2003 several hundred leaders of more than 250 Christian relief and development organizations from around the world—poverty fighters from Africa, Asia, and Latin America (with allies from the United Kingdom, Europe, and a few from the United States)—gathered in Queretaro, Mexico. Their discussions led to the creation of the "Micah Network." Inspired by the ancient Hebrew prophet to "do justice, love kindness, and walk humbly with your God," they agreed to proclaim "The Micah Challenge" to their own

> **The largest part of the work of boundary leadership is helping webs come to life, find their vital possibility, and grow.**

churches and to the government leaders in each of their countries: at issue is globalization and its impact on the poor.

Having worked in poor communities for many years, these community development agencies now turn to prophetic advocacy on behalf of the poor. To increase their impact, they have entered into a partnership with the World Evangelical Alliance (comprised of church associations in 120 countries, including the United States). That partnership will unite evangelical churches around the world (now comprising 200–400 million Christians) with evangelical relief and development organizations in the common cause of biblical justice.

Their strategy, reports Jim Wallis in *Sojourners* magazine, is "to first listen and learn from one another, promote 'integral mission'—where the proclamation and demonstration of the gospel are deeply connected so that evangelism and social justice both have clear consequences for the other—and to prophetically call upon and influence the political leaders of the world to seek justice for the poor and rescue the needy."[1]

The Micah Challenge, Wallis continues, wants extreme global poverty sliced in half by 2015. The Micah Network believes that achieving those goals will require a "spiritual engine that provides both moral energy and political accountability." The groups intend to raise "a strong evangelical voice" to political decision makers in their own countries, in wealthy nations, at the United Nations, World Bank, and other international bodies. As one delegate from a developing nation remarked quietly to Wallis, "We could be starting history in this room."[2]

Actually, he missed the point of what had already happened. Once it is proclamation time, the truly interesting transformation has already occurred. Once a web of transformation has found itself and its voice, history is well underway.

Miracles of Connectedness

There are roughly 88,000 species of trees on our little planet. As I write this looking out over a small patch of the Southern Appalachian Mountains, I can see probably fifty thousand individual trees that belong to perhaps a few hundred of those species. They look like a thick, green, breathing carpet. Thousands of other forms of life mingle among the trees' tangled roots, walking, crawling, sliding in their shade, and floating on their breath. Transformational webs are like this forest. They contain many dramatic variations, but also critical distinctions: you cannot understand a forest if you cannot see individual trees. Likewise, you cannot know community today—and certainly cannot understand or anticipate change within community—if you cannot see the webs: the spidery, shivery strands that link together the people of a place, be it a four-square-block neighborhood or a four-thousand-square-mile state.

Every single oak tree, every single pine standing on that mountainside is a miracle in its own right, adapted to its patch of sun, soil, rain, and wind. But it is a miracle that adapts within a pattern (itself miraculous) and with logic (itself miraculous). So it is with webs. Each web of transformation is certainly as complex as a forest, and certainly no less miraculous. Webs of transformation have patterns and logic that help us recognize, appreciate, care for them, and, in the process, thrive in their thriving.

 ## Profile:
James Cochrane

The word "boundary" in South Africa is anything but an intellectual concept. The sharp edges of the apartheid era enforced boundaries at every turn: in education, in housing, in employment, in health care, in religious life, at the ballot box, that did not yield their exclusionary powers until 1994. That year, change suddenly became a reality. Communities that had been seemingly silenced began to speak. Questions that had once seemed simple were now marvelously complex. Words as safe as "theological education" suddenly demanded a follow-up—theological education for whom? The church needed to discern anew how God was speaking to all of the South African people.

Enter James Cochrane. Cochrane teaches in the Department of Religious Studies at the University of Cape Town. Since the 1960s, he had been working with the anti-apartheid ecumenical church movement. After 1994 his concern turned to the role of religious life in a time of immense transition.

In 1999 he organized a "Religion in Public Life Multi Event." A series of connected events held throughout the country focused on various sectors of society, including health. The concluding seven-day conference attracted government leaders, including President Mbeki; church leaders, including the current archbishop of Cape Town; people from the South African Council of Churches, from community-based organizations, and from nongovernmental organizations (NGOs).

"We were examining religion and public life in a country where Christianity no longer has the hegemony it once did," recalls Cochrane. "We looked at policy and programs from the point of view of the church that took seriously those whose voices were normally absent or marginalized."

Each participant knew he or she needed to gather perceptions from the group to discern the doing of justice, the loving of mercy, and the walk in humility. If the transformation of society was to unfold in meaningful and healthy ways, creating opportunities for discussion and reflection was anything but academic—it was absolutely essential.

Cochrane's book, *Circles of Dignity: Community Wisdom and Theological Reflection*,[3] describes four years of work with a base ecclesial community near Durban, South Africa. These base ecclesial communities are not led by formally trained theologians. Instead, they are groups of neighbors and friends who gather to discern what God is saying to them in their particular situation. They explore what that word might be, and seek to live their lives accordingly. The Durban community, located in what is known as a "shack settlement," held a Bible study every Friday and established a primary health care program.

"The book was an attempt to reflect on their experience," says Cochrane. "What did their experience tell us about how theology is constructed by the people who are living it? And what does that say about the way we construct theology? About the way we train church leaders?"

Teaching at the University of Natal, Cochrane shaped a School of Theology that paid attention to the wisdom and experience of base ecclesial communities.

"We constructed our theological program in a number of ways," he explains. "Primarily we took into account voices that are normally shut out of the church centers, and tried to give those voices dignity. It is simply unethical not to do so. The insights of base ecclesial communities such as Durban are probably wiser and more appropriate than any expert can see. We wanted to teach clergy that they also have a body of knowledge that can be used either as power over people or as power with people. We wanted to train them to do the latter."

Bringing theological questions into the academic arena had its own set of challenges. "At first, university faculty in other disciplines didn't believe theology actually had a place in university studies, so we had to do a lot of work convincing them through the quality of our work that actually we were a center of excellence.

"Another audience was church leadership," Cochrane continues. "We did a lot of lobbying with churches and church groups to help them understand new ways of thinking about theological education.

"A third audience was all those involved in theological education in and beyond Africa. We have developed lots of international links: the Philippines, India, North America, and South America, especially Brazil.

"We were a university faculty, so we were covering a whole range of disciplines, and dealing with it in many ways. Some of us would have fit into the liberation theology model, but all of us were doing cutting edge stuff. We have been breaking boundaries."

It is perhaps ironic that the more boundaries are broken, the more their true nature appears. "It is the critical task of theology to challenge Christians to open up the cross, to go across boundaries whenever it is transforming, or at least has the potential to be transforming. Theology must challenge Christians to make interventions that would not normally be allowed. So in that sense I see boundaries as porous and flexible, and far less determined than others do.

"Boundaries are more porous because that's the way people are. One of my students interviewed some of our leading Christian activists who were tortured in detention during apartheid. He examined theology in South Africa through the context of horrific confinement. And yet these people transcended those boundaries in crucial ways. No matter how strong the boundaries, people's own agencies are far more present than we have acknowledged. Because people want to develop, they will find their way through almost impossible boundaries. It is both spiritual and practical, and it is holistic. It is about knowledge and power, and it is about the resiliency of the human spirit."

While at Natal, Cochrane and his students discarded the "deficit thinking" that focuses exclusively on what communities do not have. It did not matter that the Durban residents never had theological education, or that most had never received a high school education. They focused on the wisdom and resources that the community did have. Cochrane is taking a similar approach with the African Religious Health Assets Program, which is assessing the health needs and realities of South Africa's people.

"We're essentially saying that we are interested in what people have instead of what they don't have. No matter how little they may appear to have, we are trying to understand how that can be developed and utilized."

The people in Cochrane's web of transformation are vast: prisoners, professors and students, families in shack settlements, South African leaders, church leaders around the world, local pastors. Each is aware that he or she cannot possibly comprehend the entirety of the problem, much less the solution. They need each other.

"The process is about creating the debate. This is crucial," believes Cochrane. "I can't measure what actually comes out of it, but it has borne fruit for individuals. We are creating a network of people. I have a good friend I worked with in the anti-apartheid days and through the 1980s. He is now the secretary of the cabinet. He is trying to create a network of people, and that is what I am doing. It is a matter of making input and then drawing others into it."

As people gather together to see what can be done, they draw on their personal faith. "Over the long term, the key Scripture for me has been the verse that sums up the Law and the Prophets: Love God and neighbor as self. For me that tripartite vision—God, neighbor, and self—is the key. Most people forget the 'self' part of it, or they forget the 'neighbor' part. The dialectic between those three elements is absolutely essential."

And, for Cochrane, that is a key to the successful webs of relationships that are transforming South Africa today.

Logic, Patterns, Promises

To the right of my computer monitor I keep a snapshot I took standing on the north shore of Robben Island, looking across the choppy eight-mile channel to Cape Town, South Africa. Cape Town is many complicated and confusing layers of complicated and confusing sons and daughters of mixed hues, tangled language—a vibrant and powerful people who could never fit under the simplistic labels of white, black, mulatto. The clutter of buildings in my snapshot is dwarfed by the horizontal mass of Table Mountain rising into the mantle of clouds that catch and hold it above the city.

Robben Island is totally unremarkable, just a few square miles of low hills, scrub trees, and chalk soil washed by an unceasing but shifting breeze. Buildings of different eras mark the times when the island was a fueling station, leper colony, fort, and, most famously, the prison where Nelson Mandela spent twenty-seven years while the apartheid rulers waited for the dream of justice to blow out to sea. Today it is a museum and monument to the catalogue of cruelties, petty and profound, that in the end became part of a web of transformation. Mandela was never permitted to see this view across the strait, to even gaze on the land that held the vast diversity of Africa. Mostly he was held in the small cement prison cell, his life confined to gray bars, gray blanket, and bland food. I have touched those bars and can imagine him swinging his arms in a circle, grazing its walls in one rotation.

They did not permit Mandela to see toward shore. Why? One glance and you are reminded that for thousands of miles and hundreds of thousands of years humans have engaged one another in their differences again and again, from which emerged everything we now value. They hoped Mandela would forget and accept the despair of isolation and bitter apartness—apartheid.

Why didn't he? Why did he remain an agent of transformation? The answer is complicated and simple. He is a great man, not a common man, of course, and few of us will engage such extraordinary challenges in our boundary zones. But boundary leaders will recognize that his is a story of a great web, not just a great person. When he was invited to Oslo to receive his Nobel Prize, Mandela was asked if he wanted to bring a few close friends to the ceremony. The Norwegians were amazed when he brought several dozen—his web—which included one of his former guards! Mandela lived in a web of relationships that turned confinement into emergence, isolation into identity, powerlessness into power.

Mandela, like all boundary leaders, was formed in webs of transformation that gave him all that mattered: support, correction, protection, power, knowledge, and perspective. There is no such thing as a solitary boundary leader. Mandela tells the story of his life in the context of hundreds of other lives— people with whom he interacted in the prisons of Robben Island and other formative places.

The Robben Island prison, when Mandela was confined there, held professors, teachers, taxi drivers, clerks—a broad diversity of professionals and laborers who turned it into a university of sorts. South Africa has a highly developed system of correspondence education, so many prisoners actually received degrees via the mail; prisoners tutored each other and even guards joined in. Built to isolate and humiliate, the prison forced its "convicts" to build social networks that were resilient, intelligent, and tough. They created a web of relationships strong and smart enough to nurture the transformation of South Africa. This species of web is perfectly adapted to its tough social ecology—like the color-blind webs that birthed the U.S. civil rights movement, like the Cold War–spawned webs that crumbled the invincible Berlin wall.

As in South Africa, U.S. civil rights and East European freedom had many heroes, most of whose names we do not know. Yet it is crucial to recognize that those heroes were related to one another, connected in webs for transformation.

Not every web of relationship becomes a movement. But every movement finds its life among a web of people who seek transformation. That happens before it even has a name, because you cannot name something that is not already in motion, that is not already a social reality. John Lewis, the Atlanta congressman, was a high school student sitting in his sharecropper parents' Alabama home when he first listened to the mesmerizing words of Dr. Martin Luther King Jr. one Sunday morning on the radio. Already clear-eyed about the

oppressive reality of his dirt-road county, Lewis felt a powerful hunger for transformation. King's voice and message "sat
me bolt upright with amazement." He recognized a web of
people in which he could seek both his transformation and the
transformation of his world.

"This was the first time I had ever heard something I
would soon learn was called the social gospel—taking the
teachings of the Bible and applying them to the earthbound
problems and issues of a community and a society," Lewis
recalls in his autobiography, *Walking with the Wind.* "I was on
fire with the words I was hearing."[4]

Over the next decades, in Montgomery and in many other
mean-managed cities, Lewis would march, sing, pray—and be
beaten—with King and others in the civil rights community.
Sustained by that web of relationships, however, he found his
transformation and he saw his world transformed.

Martin Luther King did not invent the civil rights movement. It was not "his" as a company may be owned by the
entrepreneur who founded it. King played a particular and
extraordinarily vital role in it; the way he did so changed what
was possible and what in fact happened. But King, like boundary partner Lewis, was formed in a web of relationships out of
which came his remarkable capacity for language and leadership. That language, alive in his whole personality, found resonance and nurture in the whole personalities of others who,
like him, were drawn toward their own transformation and the
transformation of their world. The web of relationships
assumed outward structure and form that looked like other
organizations, for example, the Southern Christian Leadership
Conference. But the biographies of the heroes—from King to
Lewis to Vivian, Abernathy, and Carmichael—all make clear
that the transformational relationships were far more real,
vital, and resilient than the formal organizations that emerged
from them.

If you look closely at any transformational social movement, you will find its public leaders nurtured and sustained

in a web of relationships. Today, living in times so radically broken open that we see our communities as boundary zones, we are finding that a social structure—the web—makes possible a kind of leadership practice: boundary leadership. The reverse is true too: boundary leadership makes possible webs of transformation, even amid the most threatening and hostile environments.

This happens most vividly and most often in neighborhoods.

Spinning Webs

Oakhurst Baptist Church, with only a few hundred active members, has few of the attributes normally associated with power and many of those normally linked to weakness. It is in an undistinguished part of town that tends to ebb and flow in the attention of realtors. These days the neighborhood is popular among young couples and those of complicated relationships, but most of them don't go to any church at all. The location is a metaphor for the operating logic of the church, which has set up camp on the boundary zone as a web of transformational hope right in the middle of where hope is least expected.

The church is a web of transformation in a difficult city for boundary people. Even making the effort is a miracle where divisions are rampant: White from African American from Hispanic from Asian; rich from richest from poor and poorest; county from city from burbs; Baptist from Catholic from mainline Protestant from Evangelical; hospitals from public health agencies and from each other. Most pastors seem to see themselves as building ecclesiastical enclaves in which—behind which?—it is safe to hide from the swirling cold winds on the streets. Oakhurst seeks out pastoral leadership who turn this thinking inside out, looking at their congregation as a place from which to build webs of relationship linking every corner of the neighborhood. Lanny Peters has been the pastor for more than 14 years, but was preceded in the model of what should be called boundary pastoring by Mel Williams and John Nichol, which says that boundary zones are deeply etched in the church DNA.

Oakhurst spins off ministries like rich soil sprouts a forest. Some are integral to the congregation, like the recovery program across the driveway. A long list of others have found shelter in the building ranging from tutoring programs with a half dozen kids, to others that work on large scale anti-war efforts. For ten years I worked in such a ministry, *Seeds* magazine, that sprouted in the fellowship, grew into its own structure, and spread its work widely around the country. Many members work for all sorts of organizations leaning into the boundary zones issues of all sorts. I've been at Oakhurst long enough to see the pattern repeat in endlessly hopeful variations.

What is consistent among boundary leaders is the kind of relationships they tend to create for their boundary work. Great boundary pastors, like Oakhurst's, raise this to an art form. They nurture the whole social space into what Tom Munnecke calls "generative space." It is easier to see the structures and organizations that emerge from those relationships, because many create things that look like normal structures: nonprofit organizations such as the recovery center and the churches of various brands, sometimes even businesses. Indeed, the church is a swarm of such organizations, coalitions and projects. But those structures can veil the wellspring of their vitality—the powerful webs of transformation they cultivate among the visible clutter of organizations, powers, and principalities. Lanny cultivates a social ecology, not formal organization; the lines between people blur as the complexity of the social relationship emerges; in their lives and in their work, personal, interpersonal, community, and systemic transformation is all of the piece.

Whether it is bankers or immigrants without documentation, doctors or cops, architects or prostitutes, university chancellors or alcoholic professors, Lanny sees the full humanity of each individual involved in the social structures of the community. But they are not just individuals, unique and unconnected. And they are not defined only by simple identities of (un)employment, address, race, language, bank account—or any way of knowing that is static and simple. They are seen in their full humanity together and alive in webs of relationship that are complex, multilayered, and fluid. This is a good place to remember that boundary zones are—usually are!—places of danger and pain, not just transformation. People are hurt and marginalized here; frustrated and denied. Old forms of violence and power flourish even in their dying boundary zones.

Sometimes it seems enough to hope for survival; transformation can wait for later. The constant witness of those living in the recovery program is that each day has enough challenge and delight to keep the prayers—for help and thanksgiving—focused nearby. The networks in which highly vulnerable people exist—new immigrants, newly released inmates, abused women, adolescents on the run—are webs designed for survival, not transformation. The generative status of Oakhurst is that it weaves webs of relationships among survivors and those seeking transformation. This not only makes it a place of mercy, but also of justice, in that it seeks to nurture a new pattern that transforms all of those in the relationship.

Let's try and sketch the pattern of webs of transformation and then see if we can recognize a dynamic logic.

What is a web of transformation?

- It is the social structure that grows in the boundary zones.
- It is a relationship among a fairly small group of people seeking their own transformation and that of the community.
- It forms around a quest and questions, not an agenda and an answer.
- It forms at the intersection of hope and uncertainty.
- It is small because it is intimate.

- It has room for personal, interpersonal, and social transformation. It does not separate them; indeed, it lives on the synergy among the different kinds of energies.
- It is marked by relationships that reflect the adaptive and emergent vision of wholeness at the heart of the quest.
- It is marked by the quest and questions that make it live, not by what sets it apart. It lives from the center of these questions rather than being defined by its perimeter, by where it is different. It has a porous perimeter, making it is easier to know who is in than who is out.

A web of transformation is larger than can fit comfortably around a table, but is scaled for interaction. Relationships within a web of transformation may be intense and intimate, casual and collegial. Think of a room-sized group, fifteen to thirty people—up to, but very unlikely more than, two hundred. The larger the web, the more likely it is to break into smaller complementary webs. Organizational theorists note that organizations from churches to companies can function with an informal culture until they grow to about two hundred people; so too with webs.

The evidence of a web's power is not found in bigness; rather, webs are powerful because they inspire other webs and because old and new webs interweave: they become webs of webs spinning and emerging and thriving along similar quest-and-question pathways. A web lives in the creative tension between its external function, aligning community assets, and its internal work, by and among its members. The more intense the transformation underway among its members, the smaller the web; the broader its external reach, the larger it can be. But there is a limit on both ends. At some point, a too small web of influence devolves into a support group, which tends to focus on the care and tending of its participants. A too large web becomes a more anonymous form of association: an interest group or caucus without the intimacy or transparency of a web.

Much of the work of Interfaith Health Program is designed to help boundary leaders weave webs of transformation that align much larger organizational assets in communities. The web is woven between the structures (linking, for example, a church group and public health clinics), not the hard structures themselves. We need support groups, organizations, churches, coalitions, and caucuses. But a web of influence is different; it is not a named entity: not a support group, church, coalition, or caucus.

Coincidentally, biologists have noticed that given a similar ecological context, different species may adapt in similar ways, creating outward forms that make them look alike. Some species of fern have evolved into things that look a heck of a lot like trees, even though they are not. In our world of boundary zones, many forms of organization are adapting to its fluid, broken ambiguity by acting more and more like webs. And the more weblike organizations become, the more boundary leader characteristics emerge among the organization's leaders.

Convergent Webs

The convergence of movements in the information age is driven most powerfully by the nature of the problems themselves. When you look deeply and honestly at a real problem today, you see that it is part of a webwork of unsolved problems reaching far and wide into a massive system.

At this point in history, that system is the whole planet.

Paul Ray and Sherry Ruth Anderson,
The Cultural Creatives[5]

A plethora of organizations, many small and relatively informal, are beginning to understand the interrelationships of their separate agendas. After World War II, there were about two hundred NGOs working on human rights; now there are upward of ten thousand, each with a special focus: refugees, hunger, children, women, gays, indigenous peoples, disabled people, elders, those living with AIDS and their orphans. But—and this is the key development—these separate NGOs are now discovering that their work gains insight, potential, and power in relationship with others. "The urgent need for solutions calls for a further interweaving as the movements look for ever-more compelling rationales for their work," argue Ray and Anderson. "As they do, they become more similar—not in their programs but in their language, their diagnoses of the problems, and their assumptions about the underlying causes."

Movements converge, drawn by similar analysis of specific problems toward a yet-to-be-realized commonality of solutions. Viewed close up, that convergence is ragged and conflicted, of course, at times two streams flowing smoothly together, but at other times and places like rocks beneath a glacier coming together only after being ground to dust.

We see this convergence happen during almost every run of the Institute for Public Health and Faith Collaborations. One critical exercise the teams experience is to take the life of one person and draw the spiral of their brokenness. The teams move into the particularity of the life, as best they can, feeling themselves on sacred ground. The particularity of the lives usually draws the teams beyond the initial name of the problem that first attracted their attention: AIDS, obesity, diabetes and such. In moving deeply into the individual, they find themselves drawn toward surprisingly common ground with the other teams that may have started with quite a different problem. This becomes even more radically evident when we ask them to try to draw the spiral the other way—to imagine what could have been done by relevant people within compassion range of the life. When teams looked up from their own pictures, they realized they were converging with the other teams' visions.

In substance, what those different leaders from different experiences, different backgrounds, and different work environments drew looked surprisingly similar; quickly they found common bonds: they could identify with others' lives and talk together about the intersections of their hopes. The visions that emerged, whether the participants were from Wisconsin, North Carolina, New York, or Montana, described the same world, for a broad range of relationship, vision, and commitment—viewpoints conscious and subconscious—link those leaders and thereby link their various movements. These are people who dare to rethink old positions and question the conventional wisdom of previous generations. In reinterpreting the past to give the present meaning and the future direction, they create webs exactly at the confluence of the many movements underway today.

Convergence of such complex social processes requires relationships capable of holding a great deal of highly emotive and intellectual complexity; knowledge and passion flow together. The "container" for that powerful brew is found only in the human relationship, not the abstract idea. Relationships can carry much greater information in more comprehensible form than any verbal language. Standing for ten minutes with a mother living with AIDS and her soon-to-be-orphaned children in an African village creates a relationship to the full complexity of the catastrophe that could never find expression in words.

One does not need a web of transformation simply for personal growth or (worse) mere professional development. It is much easier to look for less demanding relationships such as courses or special interest groups. Or, if one is wounded enough to need repair, it may be more appropriate to seek a support group.

Webs of transformation emerge where they have to emerge at the time they simply must. Webs of transformation are about action. They are spun when people, seeking answers to nagging, gnawing, won't-turn-loose questions, begin to reach out for solutions because they have no choice but to reach out. Unless—and until—powered by overwhelming demands, webs of transformation are far too much trouble, too disturbing and intrusive, to justify the time and energy their development requires.

Drawn like a bird sailing on the breath of the forest, people are liberated to create new patterns of progress. They discover that the assets they have guarded and hoarded can and should be realigned with those of others to create a much more sensitive, stable, and significant impact.

The relationships in the web often illuminate surprising implications and uses of the assets. Assets can be social as well as financial, cultural as well as formal. Embedded in skills and knowledge both formal and casual, assets are what we have to work with in the work of transformation: money, skill, energy, and talent. The assets that might call forth a web of transformation—and in turn be used by the web's members—are relevant to

Webs form at the confluence of opportunity and concern, where things are in sufficient motion to suggest that transformation is wanting to happen.

the future (not necessarily the past) of the members of the web; to the community, however they might experience it; and to the quest they share. Webs form at the confluence of opportunity and concern, where things are in sufficient motion to suggest that transformation is wanting to happen.

 Profile:
Mimi Kiser

Mimi Kiser, associate director of IHP, coordinates the Institute for Public Health Faith Collaborations that is funded by the Center for Disease Control. She selects and invites teams from around the United States to come together for five days to hone the skills required to lessen health disparities in the United States. Before they arrive, she has spent endless hours in preparation. Her ability to plan and coordinate such events is second to none. But that is not what sets her apart.

Her gift is the capacity to extend a call to colleagues that is fundamentally spiritual. She involves the heart as well as the mind of all who attend—an exploration into selfhood that she first experienced as a student working on her master's in public health.

She joined with five Presbyterian churches that were sponsoring a weekend retreat on sexuality for junior high schoolers. With careful planning, they set an agenda that included gender identity, not just information; genuine relationships, not just surface images.

Today when Kiser speaks to groups about public health disparities, she often shares this experience of "opening together of the heart and the mind that really shifted my life."

"The weekend was very well thought out, its leaders were very loving and supportive of the kids," she says. "As Howard Thurman said, transformation is a matter of the 'head' and the 'heart.' During that weekend, I listened, felt, heard, and experienced something that was personally transforming. Along with those kids, I heard and felt the message, 'God loves you as a female; God loves you as a male.' I had never heard that message before in such a deep way. I grew up in the '50s and '60s where, at least in my environment, the message about being a woman was not a very positive one. So the weekend was very healing and soothing for me personally.

"And then I had a 'head reaction' about the environment we created for those kids. I started thinking about the meaning and values that so positively supported their human gender identity development. I thought about the social structures and entire networks of social structures in the country. I realized that they had the potential to create this kind of an environment.

"I also knew from my public health training that the decisions people make based on their sense of who they are as male and female have vast implications. It is really beyond the scope of the human mind to calculate the social costs of what we might call unwise decisions—whether it's sexually transmitted diseases, or abusive partner relationships, or unintended pregnancies. I realized that HIV/AIDS transmission, for example, comes largely out of that sense of who we are. I saw the importance of creating opportunities as we did that weekend. It was almost like a gate opening in my vocational life."

In the language of boundary leadership, that vocation became a "call to colleagues." This call asks colleagues to link their personal faith with professional concern. In the training sessions, equal time is spent sharing personal lives and thinking critically about systems in need of change. The entire event resists focusing on either "heart" or "mind" exclusively. The two work together.

"I love the part of the Institute which involves selecting the team, putting them together with other teams, selecting the mentors and the presenters and the consultants. I love figuring out who might work well together," Kiser says. "Each event is a kind of emerging possibility. Each one brings together a combination of who people are, what their struggles may be, what their gifts are. There is something generative in all of this. I try to sense what is possible when people come together."

The final night, participants often gather in a circle and those who wish to speak share what they have learned. One pastor has come to a better sense of his ordination. A public health worker has been reminded of how important his work actually is. There are laughs . . . and tears.

The next morning, each team describes its plans, strategies, and goals to improve conditions at home. The deeply personal has found its social implications, and the social implications have drawn strength from a community well.

"It is important that we create space that nurtures people, space that affirms and allows them to recognize and strengthen what they are doing," Kiser says. "When we do that well, there is a great deal of energy for change.

"The boundary zones are places of risk and transformation. And they provide space to connect with other people. These spaces allow a greater possibility for something new. There is a kind of resonance that is both healing and whole. In such a place,

there is less possibility for oppression and inequality and alien-
ation and disenfranchisement. There is less fear. We are separate,
distinct creatures, but we sense our full humanity, and as we do,
we find God."

Webs for a Jumping Universe

One of the findings of science I like best is that living systems
do not slowly evolve from one form to another: this is as true
in human evolution as in physics. A static period is suddenly
broken by change fast and deep. The smallest systems we can
track, electrons in their spinning, do not make smooth transi-
tions from one phase to another as energy is added. They jump
suddenly from one orbit to the next; quarks spin one way, then
suddenly the other way. The postmodern architect Charles
Jencks says this demands an architecture fit for a "jumping
universe."[6] I do not know if I want my buildings jumping, but
even a glance at the newspaper tells me that we need relationships—webs—that can jump.

Large systems, likewise, flip and jump in relatively brief
periods of time, especially when facing multiple intersecting
challenges to the old forms and logic. The interwoven nature
of our problems and opportunities is creating a convergence of
movements that is profound and powerful.

Webs of transformation emerge where the world is trying
to jump. Today the world wants to jump much more than we
are prone to expect. For example, the catastrophe of AIDS in
Africa, like storm clouds whirling into hurricane force, is creating the pressure for numerous webs that can make possible
the chasm-crossing jump.

We have done some research at IHP that indicates that
current efforts to combat AIDS among orphans in Africa are
well below $200 million per year. The amount is rising gradu-
ally, but not sufficiently: Africa needs a jump.

By 2010 there will be more than twenty million HIV/AIDS-related orphans in Africa. A meaningful improvement in efforts to alter the horrible conditions and inadequate care of HIV/AIDS-related orphaned children alone requires a roughly hundredfold increase in effort by the end of 2008, and maintenance of that level of support for decades or more. If organizations such as Save the Children, Child Reach, and the Christian Children's Fund are correct, roughly $300 per child in annual outside support, appropriately employed, will make a significant improvement in their situations. (I can barely type such an absurd figure, knowing that my daughter spends that much on music CDs in a year.) Even this scandalous penury means a total of $6 billion will be required annually. This is about 40 percent of the cost of one cup of Starbucks latte—that's $1.10, please—for each of the 104.5 million American households per week. But moving that amount of funds requires a level of relationship that cannot be achieved with a typical rational ramp. We need a jump.

As I was writing this book IHP was asked to see how such a jump might be sparked among people of faith in the United States. After a bit of scouting, we noticed that nearly every religious organization big enough to have a web site had said pretty much what one would want them to say about helping the orphans. But every number in every one of their plans was missing a zero: they hoped for $6 million and it should have been $60 million; they projected 3 years, which everyone knows must be 30 years.

The zero was hidden beneath the grown-ups' failure to imagine seriously. Their imaginations were capable of such deep and irrelevant slumber because they were buffered from both catastrophe and possibility. Imagination breathes relationship; transformation jumps from relationships.

AIDS and the catastrophe of AIDS orphans are a complex, multilayered reality. One cannot go even two steps toward simple mercy without landing in very deep water roiled by centuries of oppressive efforts to break African family and village forms. Racial injustice, colonial marginalization, more racial injustice, global financial patterns, domination systems covering patent rights for pharmaceuticals and trade flows—and more racial prejudice—only begin the description.

To show even the least possible kindness toward the orphans of AIDS, one must take on the captivity of African villages to the global systems in which their poverty and marginalization is perpetuated. The religious dynamics are a whole thicket of their own. European and American religious groups have long-standing links to Africa, of course, but not always entirely noble ones. Missionaries served in many cases as the velvet glove on the colonial fist. As a result, the fastest growing religious groups are not connected to Western churches. They are Muslim and, increasingly, a vast network of Christian groups that are loosely linked under the umbrella of "Africa Instituted Churches." Nevertheless, the scale, duration, and complexity of the orphan crisis, not to mention those at risk of AIDS and those living (and dying) with AIDS, draws all concerned, from Muslim to evangelical Christian, onto a common ground that defies any of our existing frameworks of understanding and relationship.

Simply linking our various existing ideas and assets cannot solve the challenges embedded in HIV/AIDS. Animating and aligning resources on this scale demands transformation. Making a difference requires a massive jump in imagination and response. This will not happen without webs of relationships at the point of our confluence: they, and they alone, can make that jump possible. For what is being transformed is not just our external giving, but our internal understanding of our world; not just our relationship to orphans far away, but to one another in our complexity nearby.

It is exactly wrong to hope for change one person at a time: the changes are too slow, small, and fragile. The world needs jumps, which only happen one web at a time.

Christian Connections for International Health (CCIH) is another example of the webs emerging around AIDS, partly because most of its members come from traditional organizational cultures rooted in the U.S. Protestant denominations. It has a board of directors, an executive director, annual meetings, a newsletter, a web site (ccih.org), and a Washington, D.C., address that gets it invited to numerous power meetings. It has almost no money whatsoever and zero command authority. Nobody has to do anything it says about anything.

CCIH's leverage of influence among the nation's movers and shakers is a web of transformation spun together by the tenacious desire to be faithful to what the organization understands God to be trying to do in the world, especially for the poor. Its members are committed to one another and to the possibilities of systematically showing mercy and justice. Hence CCIH members engage their own denominations and organizations and institutions such as the World Bank, the United Nations, and the structures of U.S. government. The webs they weave around large organizational assets attach at the heart, but lead directly to the brain.

The crisis of AIDS, magnified as it is in Africa by layers of race and oppression, exemplifies the boundary zone and the emergence of webs of transformation. Webs are new relationships not defined or contained by blood, orthodoxy, nation, ethnicity, or economics. Generally, webs emerge after simpler forms of organization (within those identities) have failed to manage the complexity of the challenge. AIDS orphans in Africa are a white-light blinding instance of status-quo failure; those lonely and desperate children make absolutely impossible—if conditions are to be changed and lives are to be saved—any idea of gradual ramps and merely rational plans. All has shattered and broken open, leaving almost nothing functional in the boundary zones—nothing . . . except those shimmering, glittering, fragile webs of transformation.

Finding Webs

Jumps—and webs of transformation—happen amid crisis, discontinuity, disruption; they are quantum leaps of scale, scope, and complexity. Look for structural failures, breakdowns of old roles, the loss of coherent meaning, and the collapse of power into violence or active oppression. In the vacuum of meaning, responses can jump up or down: up toward coherence, downward into cacophony.

Expect to see webs emerging:

- at dissident edges, where dissent and discomfort are engaging the powers, and the voices are finding one another;
- at learning edges, where disruptive knowledge and new capacities are beginning to penetrate and undermine older paradigms;
- at organizational edges, where those who have been pushed to the margins are finding one another;
- at the edges of meaning, where deep and disruptive questions blend with new symbols of reversal, hope, and lament; and we find ourselves among others discovering symbols and language at the depths of our soul.

Where Roles Are Changing

The place to begin a search for transformative webs is in our own lives. As we move beyond the margins of old structures, we find our way toward new and more useful expectations. Our work changes, and with it our roles and relationships change.

The more exposed one is to the chaos of community, the more likely it is that the old boundaries that defined competence, knowledge, skills, and professional networks are melting in the hot fire of what Scott Russell Sanders earlier called "the burning earth." The edges between adjacent skills and roles melt, fade, then disappear altogether. Look for webs to emerge among those trying to cope, and even more among those who are moving toward the new identities with a sense of liberation, curiosity, and openness. Something new is happening to us that may be more lively and vital than our old identities; we are being aligned with the strengths and purposes that called us into our roles in the first place.

Not without some grief for the old simple days of administering immunization programs, many public health leaders are realizing they should be nurturing healthy communities by energizing and mobilizing all and any structures that can promote health. These radically different expectations quickly suggest the need for new skills, for different capacities.

One web that has been transformational for public health leaders is the Public Health Leadership Society (PHLS). The several hundred PHLS members all complete an intensive year-long institute designed to build their leadership capacities. All have significant responsibilities for major county and state health departments. Most manage organizations with hundreds of employees and millions of dollars in public funds with explicit legal responsibilities for disease surveillance as well as food and water inspection. They are, of course, the very front lines of preparations for bioterrorism and other catastrophic things most of us do know enough about to fear.

In 1998 PHLS's president was Paul Weisner, who heads up my home county's health department. Paul, a veteran of every level of public health administration, knew that public health leaders by themselves were not capable of creating the conditions for optimal quality of life, no matter how large or sophisticated their budgets and programs. The job—the very identity—of public health leaders had to shift from its administrative focus to one of facilitating transformation. Changing roles demanded new skills and understandings. Public health leaders needed to learn from others in the community who shared their sense of possibility and their hope for a renewed community. Because he is a boundary leader, Paul developed a strategy of "spanning" PHLS toward two key leadership groups: those in the arts and those in faith.

As is almost always true, other parts of the web were already reaching from the other direction to make connections much more quickly than one would think possible. In 1999 IHP and PHLS convened a retreat to explore ways to "deepen and accelerate" the convergence of faith and public health. Mimi Kiser, IHP associate director, and Paul wove a web on a loom of phone calls, careful selection of participants and intensive meeting design. Twenty-six people, balanced roughly between those working in public heath and those representing religious groups, attended.

Over the course of our three-day meeting, we spoke of our pain, frustration, anger, and shame at how we had failed to live up to what we believed and hoped for. We talked about the transformation happening in our work, our worlds, our personal lives. And we sketched a way of helping each other on all those levels.

Webs do not just talk; they act. One visible product of our time together was a statement of values and common goal. Today that "call to colleagues" lives on the IHP web site (www.ihp-net.org/joincolleagues), where it has been signed by hundreds of others around the world who resonate with its vision and ideals. The call also became the foundational inspiration for the Institute for Public Health and Faith Collaborations, an IHP program that emerged from the call's challenges. It also informed a multimillion-dollar "Strong Partners" initiative linking ten religious foundations with the federal government and several dozen faith-based organizations. None of this was anticipated in its specifics. All this emerged because people sought a web of relationships in which they could explore transformations in their roles as public and religious leaders.

How is your role changing? Are you finding that you need new skills to enable you to meet new kinds of demands, language, and people? It is likely that webs of interrelationships are already emerging on the edges of your social and professional networks.

Among New Structures

Webs are designed to thrive amid instability. Thus you find them where people are engaging complex community dynamics to create something truly new. Webs tend to form where relationships, often among new partners gathered for a specific task, produce fertile ground for understanding and engaging complex problems. A web is especially helpful among diverse partners whose different languages, structures, meanings, outlooks, and symbols make closeness paramount.

Webs often occur when old structures need rebirth. About a century ago, the Parliament of the World's Religions was formed from the optimistic democratic model then in vogue. Religions were sort of like nations; their representatives gathered, debated, even negotiated (in gentlemanly fashion) with one another. People were identified by their religion and were expected to function within the framework of its tenets.

But religions are not nations. And a religion's adherents seldom act in patterns predictable from their written codes and proclamations. Some are almost identical with their geographical home culture, others are highly adaptable; some are formed mostly of ideas, others of behaviors, others around rituals. Still, it was, and continues to be, a good idea for religions' leaders to gather in the same room now and then to talk.

But the outcome of those large-scale discussions can never produce anything like the initiatives of a group like the United Religions Initiative (URI). Organized using the revolutionary insights of David Cooperrider of Case Western Reserve University, URI was convened by Bishop Bill Swing of San Francisco. It emerged among a highly diverse group of people—a web if there ever was one—who were moved deeply by the failure of religious powers to deal with ethnic violence and its closely linked global challenges. Over a period of a couple years of discussion, which included personal and organization transformation, URI took form based on a radically different organizational logic of "cooperation circles." Cooperrider knew that organizations thrive when they are allowed to move toward their vital heart. The art of the cooperation circle is born when diverse people appreciate a radical new possibility around which energy and commitment form with speed and beauty, just as when a string is dropped in a glass of sugar water. There are now upward of a thousand such circles around the world;

they come in many different sizes, but all are defined much as I describe webs of transformation: each circle emphasizes transformation, each promotes a functional vision of accomplishing something transformative, whether mundane or bold. The action that is the visible magnet for the group is expected to be sustained by a quality of relationships among the members in which they can experience their own transformation too.

URI was born at the millennium in California. It is the web logic of transformation, not the Parliament logic of negotiation. It thinks in terms of filaments, not bricks; in forms for action, not talk. Yet they may be moving toward each other: the Parliament of the World's Religions is increasingly adapting itself to web logic, moving far away from nation-state metaphors as it approaches global gatherings. And URI constantly struggles to understand what kind of centralized administrative functions a web of webs requires in the global boundary zone.

Webs are more interesting than the structures they spin off. But a great place to look for webs of transformation is where new structures are emerging. Look behind the structure to see who spins the threads that spawn the structure. What is the source of their vitality, their vision? Go look and see.

Where New Visions Are Emerging

A universe that wants to jump prods us toward new relationships, new patterns of thinking, toward surprising discourse, symbols. People instinctively gather around hope, even when it is articulated incompletely.

For years, my church has encouraged a process of "sounding a call" when a member feels drawn toward a new ministry. She or he comes to the congregation during the worship service and shares that vision. Those for whom the call resonates then gather down front by the piano, and it is usually an odd ensemble, with a surprising range of ages, economic statuses, and backgrounds. They schedule a first meeting—itself a difficult task in our busy lives—and then, over a process of weeks, months, and even years, they plan the actions needed to turn hope into reality. Even when the vision sounds specific ("Let's form a homeless shelter"), it turns out that people come with pieces of a dream that may or may not fit together, that may or may not make any sense at all. Sometimes the web is stillborn. But often puzzle pieces do fit diverse personalities, ideas become actions, and a dream is born with startling clarity and beauty: a homeless shelter, a tutoring program, a food pantry.

Across town, another sort of web gathers every Monday at a local restaurant. The Concerned Black Clergy has an agenda focused on listening: to ideas, visions, plots, and schemes that are looking for webs of people to give them flesh and form. Political campaigns, protest movements, and immunization efforts—a thousand good ideas and maybe twice that many bad ones—emerge here. If you are looking for an "organization," you may be disappointed (it runs pretty ragged). But if you look for a web, you will see the Concerned Black Clergy's extraordinary record of transformation.

Scholars and researchers who are trying to engage the complexity of human challenges tend to create another kind of web. The Africa Religious Health Assets Project, mentioned earlier, developed amid a community of scholars and field experts seeking to create a systematic knowledge base of religious health assets in sub-Saharan Africa. Their goal in assembling this information was not particularly academic, however: they wanted to use the facts they uncovered to "align and enhance the work of religious health leaders and public policy decision-makers in their collaborative effort to meet the challenge of disease such as HIV/AIDS, and to participate in the creation of health, especially for those in poverty."[7]

In short, this web of relationships is helping transform thinking into doing; relationships are building trust and commitments among people as distant from one another as Norway, the United States, and a number of African countries. The process demands a web because it cannot be done within the lines of any set of simple disciplinary discourses. United are anthropologists, theologians of several stripes, medical and public health professions, economists, and field program leaders. Each is already drawn to the boundaries of his or her formal discipline and each is ready, indeed, needing a way of going deeply with those in complementary fields.

The result: a web of transformation. Such webs do not make for merely smart discussion producing more clever theory and better data. They make possible that rare event: intellect and passion aligned beyond calculation toward the decisions and commitments that lead toward life.

Look for other such webs in places where thinkers are following their most powerful questions into the complexity of the boundary zones. Vital questions demand a web of relationships in which the frustrating and awkward work of creating new conceptual containers can occur. Look to the edges of disciplines where thoughtful people talk about reality. Look where senior scholars are willing to risk interdisciplinary discourse or where young scholars refuse to be dominated by too-small and too-confined disciplines.

Or just look down toward the front of the church, where that small group is forming, or over at the corner booth in that restaurant.

Where Collaborative Tools Are Used to Engage Power

Boundary zones may be fluid, but they are not abstract. Many boundary leaders spend much of their time in committee meetings doing the work of, well, committing and seeking new commitments. Sometimes committees never go beyond mechanical decisions: event planning, goal setting, report giving. Sometimes they do.

My daughter Lauren noticed that our little city of Decatur had never observed Earth Day. She decided it was time that it should. She began contacting organizations and groups who needed to help. The vast majority of time was spent on permits, tables for artists, microphones for singers, permission slips for the children's choir—and portable toilets.

But sometimes something more happens, especially if a boundary leader knows what to look for. Sometimes people come together and recognize the possibility of deeper collaboration. At Earth Day, the people who came because of trees, birds, recycling, bicycles, children, rivers, and a nice day in the sun found one another. At least some of them did.

A boundary leader knows to look for those places where the tools of collaboration are being used: committees, contracts, agreements, and common spaces. A boundary leader can recognize a web of transformation trying to emerge beneath all the clutter.

On the opposite end of the scale of size—from Decatur to Seattle—is the web of webs of transformation that spun around the 1999 meeting of the World Trade Organization (WTO). Great concentration of power can generate great webs of relationships to oppose it.

The WTO meeting should have been, if those danged webs had not intervened, another gray snore of a meeting among gray global bureaucrats negotiating gray trade accords. Instead, the barricades were stormed by fifty thousand protesters, not from one or two but from hundreds of networks. It was a web of webs that erupted into view at the point of engagement with a nearly unaccountable form of global power.

As Ray and Anderson describe it in *Cultural Creatives:*

In some ways, the battle in Seattle felt just like the 1960s protests of the black freedom movement and the antiwar movement. But the protesters had deftly used the Internet to get organized, and they managed to carry protest to the next octave by combining it with zany celebrations to draw media attention. The convergence of interests and organizations caught almost everyone by surprise.

Dressed as sea turtles and monarch butterflies, death's heads and victims of violence, fifty thousand activists showed up from around the world. Ecologists and feminists, Teamsters and steelworkers in union jackets, witches and nuns, consumer and health advocates, native people, human rights activists, and people against multinationals and globalization came prepared to engage in the great ritual drama—parading and shouting slogans, linking arms to block streets and buildings, getting arrested and going limp, and finally being dragged off to jail.[8]

With their extraordinary webbing of different groups whose primary orientation ranged across the spectrum of human-rights, religious, and economic interests, the Seattle protests challenged basic functions and authorities of the WTO. It was a web exposing and opposing the complex implications and behavior of the WTO.

When webs are linked to other webs, the emergent possibilities are numberless.

The way the groups were linked was filament logic, not brick logic; web, not parliament.

Here, revealed on TV screens and newspaper front pages, was the power of webs when linked to other webs. As we have noted, one web would encompass only a few people. But just because each is small and personal does not mean that united they cannot scale to global dimensions, as many fleeting clouds can build into the furious power of a thunderstorm.

When webs are linked to other webs, the emergent possibilities are numberless. The relationship among webs is limited only by the relationship among those possibilities. This means the number and interrelationship of webs of influence is beyond the capacity of anyone to track, much less control.

The nature of webs of transformation has profound implications for the nature of the organizations and structures that find themselves on the edge of or in the boundary zone.

5

A Word for One Another

We try to pack in a few worthwhile things between birth and death, and quite often succeed. It is, however, hard to achieve anything significant if, as in sub-Saharan Africa, the median age at death is less than five years. . . . Having made it beyond those early years, it may be difficult for us to imagine how restricted a life so many of our fellow human beings lead, what little living they manage to do. There is, of course, the wonder of birth (impossible to recollect), some mother's milk (sometimes not), the affection of relatives (often thoroughly disrupted), perhaps some schooling (mostly not), a bit of play (amid pestilence and panic), and then things end (with or without a rumble). The world goes on as if nothing much has happened.
Amartya Sen, Foreword to *Pathologies of Power*

In the end, what is the significance of boundary leadership? Will it be enough to save a troubled neighborhood, let alone an imperiled planet? Is it worthwhile? At the boundaries, the light is often too bright to bear, the shadows too deep to penetrate. So it is not ours to say if boundary leadership will "work" better than old-fashioned inside-the-walls management. The strengths may not be enough, the webs too weak to hold. Maybe we will have been the last generation that could have hoped to reverse the drift toward permanent damage to a planet, a catastrophic shredding of its natural systems.

Yet experience with boundary leaders makes me think it is too early to give up on the planet. Boundary leadership is a claim against the obvious momentum of "the powers." A claim, in other words, that moves through, but beyond, the data: a claim of faith.

Boundary leaders find each other in the webs of relationships drawn to the places of great fear and great hope, especially where the different specialized streams of activity resonate and converge with others. When boundary leaders meet in webs of transformation, they do not seem desperate, as one might expect when adding up the long lists of pathologies. Old management would count, analyze, list, prioritize, plan, and sequence each of the pathologies, developing a case for despair in the process. Boundary leaders do all those things, but that is not the way they live, not the heart of their capacity to lead.

Boundary leadership is a spiritual practice. This is the simplicity at the heart of the living complexity. Although boundary leaders draw on a broad range of skills and competencies, the way of leadership is not understood by its social or rational techniques. We borrow language that is only partly helpful in describing the simple integrity at the heart. Boundary leaders find life coherent because it is integral, lived as a whole in which the components are connected. Indeed, commitments to family, community, the planet, God, and oneself are so connected as to be singular and seamless. This singularity is the radical gift that changes all the plethora into One.

Boundary Spirituality

Thee Smith, my teacher and friend at Emory's Department of Religion, penetrates deeply into the nature of violence, including that between religious groups. He says that the roots of violence between religions must be answered not by going away from religion, but by going deeper into religion. Each faith tradition has a dangerous and a safe stream within it. It is the profound duty of those of us living within any faith tradition to nurture the stream of spirituality that is safe for others. Likewise, every religion has a stream that encourages a withdrawal from complexity and a stream that seeks its highest expression in the spirit of hope, generosity, and justice that is inclusive. Most religions honor as the highest virtue a preferential hospitality for those who are different. I do not know enough about how this trait is developed in other religions, although I know I have experienced it as a recipient of such hospitality in the homes and places of worship of Muslims, Buddhists, Hindus, and Baha'is. We find ourselves at a common well of reverence.

> **Boundary leadership is a claim against the obvious momentum of "the powers."**

We move—together—beyond leadership technique to the formation of reverence for complex emergence at every scale from personal to systemic. As we do, we move on a path with predictable spiritual challenges. Spirituality is often spoken of as if it were a source of simple motivation, inspiration, and encouragement. In the boundary zone faith is a field of profound questions. Like disparities and our web of relationships, the questions draw us beyond our simple identities and tribal answers in ways that feel like life. There is a pattern that people of any theological tradition must encounter in their own way. My own map of faith challenges looks something like figure 5.

This is not an entirely happy map to be on, for it demands much that I do not have in terms of intellectual and spiritual depth and range. I am only partly encouraged to realize that others from other faith traditions have similar maps, certainly in their key branches. To advance on this journey, I imagine spiritual competencies that make possible the transformations envisioned by the public health leaders we looked at in the last chapter. It is wise to distrust precision in spiritual things, for it seems too easy to lop off the mystery to fit our attention span and comfort. But a map of the spiritual competencies I would wish for myself at this point in my young transformation looks something like figure 6.

Imagine the two maps overlaid, as one might overlay a geophysical map with one of roads and towns. They describe the same journey in the same space, the boundary zone. The first shows the terrain, maybe even vegetation, where the water runs. One can discern the difficulty of moving from here to there (from questions of Home to Pluralism to Power). But on any given Monday morning, a road map may be more helpful, as it suggests where to turn next. So the map of spiritual competencies suggests a pathway amid the big questions. The map is still quite short of a syllabus or packing list for the journey. It is embarrassing to offer it up at all, given the pretension of mapping a journey on which I am only a few steps down the path. It is sure to be like those curious maps the early explorers drew of North America with bays and rivers exaggerated all out of scale. But like those, it is better to put down for all to see the (flawed) map that is in our head so that others who cross the same territory can correct it.

The map of boundary zone spiritual competencies begins with illuminating the pathways from personal to social and back. This is the step toward the transformational relationships that draw us into the deep water and make it possible to swim there. This is far more than a rational, analytical process. I trace my faith tradition at least to the early-twentieth-century movement of religious social progressives called the Social Gospel. The leading voice of that movement, Walter Rauschenbusch, wrote books of political analysis and was heavily involved in the turbulence of urban labor movements. But he also wrote a book of "prayers for the social awakening" to develop a spirituality fit for the social movements—I dare say spiritual competence. It reflects something of the whole "system" of spirituality, toward

Figure 5

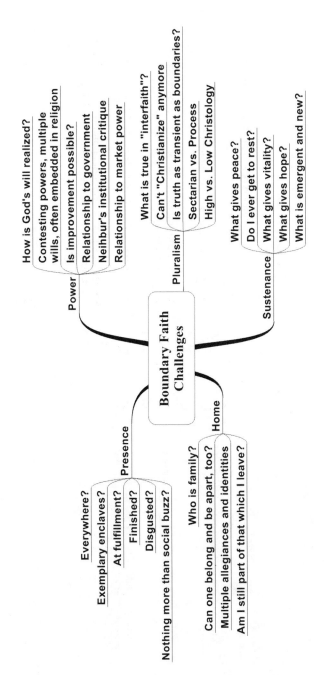

Figure 6

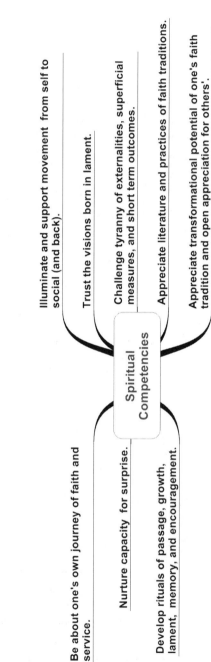

which we are still growing, a spirituality not so easily over-
whelmed among those of us who know too much about the
world. For example, Rauschenbusch prays:

> O God, we pray thee for all whose vigor is being drained by
> slow and wasting illness. Strengthen their powers as they bat-
> tle for their life, and if it be possible, we beseech thee to restore
> them and grant them the fulness of their years. If their strength
> is failing, give them courage still to labor cheerfully and to
> leave to those who love them dear memories of faith and
> patience for the distant days.[1]

If Rauschenbusch's prayer stopped here, any boundary
leader would choke. To Paul Farmer, it seems that there is
more than mercy and complaint to offer. As Farmer notes:

> What do all of these victims have in common? Not language
> or gender or political views; not religion or race or ethnicity.
> What they share, all of them, is poverty and, generally, an
> unwillingness to knuckle under. Pathologies of power damage
> all concerned—and who isn't concerned?—but kill chiefly the
> poor. These crimes are the symptoms and signs of structural
> violence. Indeed, when we regard the perpetrators of these
> crimes from any comfortable reserve, it is important to recall
> that with our comfort comes a loss of innocence, since we
> profit from a social and economic order that promises a body
> count. That is, surely there are direct and causal relationships
> between a protected minority enjoying great ease and those
> billions who go without the bare necessities of food, shelter,
> potable water, and medical services? Pathologies of power are
> also symptoms of surfeit—of the excess that I like as much as
> the next guy.
> How do we, as the lingo would have it, "process" such
> abominable contiguity? Our best hope, it sometimes seems, is
> oblivion. Let the world's endless jeremiad be blotted out by
> action films and other entertainments, sport-utility vehicles,

high irony, identity politics that erase the world's pool or struggles for personal advancement within this or that institution. Choose your poison; choose your anesthesia. Help yourself. Soon we will all be too old for justice, anyway.[2]

We need the spiritual capacity to seek and trust the visions that emerge from lament so that we move through complaint, then beyond, finding strength to continue working and hoping. In fact, Rauschenbusch's prayer continued:

Since we are all jointly guilty of the conditions which have bred their disease, may we stand by those who bear the burden of our common sin, and set the united will of our community against this power that slays the young and strong in the bloom of their life. May this death that creeps from man to man be a solemn reminder that we are all one family, bound together in joy and sorrow, in life and death, that we may cease from our selfish indifference and together seek thy kingdom and thy righteousness which will bring us health and life.[3]

Rauschenbusch was praying in the context of Tuberculosis Day, at the time widely observed by churches in the United States, rather like many of us today observe special days for the environment or HIV/AIDS. Rauschenbusch helps us move from appropriate mercy toward justice, which includes, when we least expect it, *us*. We move from self, to the whole, and back. Tuberculosis is not gone from the world and still well worth praying for. The boundary zone knows of many "slow and wasting" phenomena that bring us to our knees, or should.

Boundary zone spirituality prays with eyes wide open to the powers and their inevitable careless brutality, their complacency that makes disparities intractable. This is a kind of spiritual practice that challenges tyranny of externalities, superficial measures, and short-term outcomes—those things that act like anesthetics, or hallucinogens—in the boundary zones. Farmer, like anyone who sustains a life of engagement with pathological power, lives in a web of relationships that sustain one another. When we gather boundary leaders, spiritual practices include prayer, song, silence, and testimony, which create a tapestry of sustaining faith. It is more like a healthy stew than an outline of a systematic theology. It holds complexity, lament, and hope without reducing it to its components.

Ritual, Reverence, and Reality

A boundary leader's spiritual competence rests on the ability to recognize God in the moment of surprise. There is something deeply spiritual in a mature expectation of the new, the unexpected, the unanticipated. This capacity is rooted in reverence for the capacity of the system to create amid shattered pieces. As William Sloane Coffin says,

> But if doubts are important, wonder is all-important. None of us scoffs at the stars, nor do we sneer at sunsets. Yet we depreciate so much else; it seems almost inevitable that, as civilization advances, the sense of wonder declines. We forget that both the tree of life and the tree of knowledge are deeply rooted in the soil of mystery. The most incomprehensible fact is the fact that we comprehend at all.
>
> And wonder is not reserved for beauty alone; it has an ethical dimension, it leads to reverence. And what an irony it is that just as technology frees us to be fully human—not mere survivors of the earth's rigors, but thinking, feeling human beings—how ironic, and savagely so, that soon we may lose the whole planet because we have lost our sense of wonder. For finally, only reverence can restrain violence, violence against nature, violence against one another.[4]

How is reverence developed? It is a gift of relationship, received in relationship that opens beyond itself like a path leading away from home. The relationships that nurture the capacity for surprise and reverence are found by moving on one's own journey of faith and service. We are constantly confirmed in the simple confidence that our lives are not wasted when we, as Collin Morris says, "grab the near edge of a great problem and act at some cost to ourselves."[5] We have only to glance to notice that many hands lie alongside ours. But simple aggregation of effort is not necessarily illuminating or reverential. The key is to be with people who also understand their journey as one surprising personal and social transformation. It may be more intuitive to seek reverence in the private, silent spaces. But that is a counsel of despair for boundary leaders who live suspended in webs of numerous relationships.

In *Unconquerable World,* Jonathan Schell examines the life of Mahatma Gandhi as an example of what I would recognize as boundary leadership on a continental scale. Like other boundary leaders, he was forced outside the lines of existing theories of change because he saw the impossibility of success for those oppressed and denied by power that could not be conquered violently. Gandhi's power was rooted, Schell recognizes, in spiritual practices. "In order to drive the gun out of politics he had to invite God in."[6] A boundary leader, Gandhi had complex hopes and a strategy of engagement that avoided classic political schemes based on coercion. The strategy of positive engagement, poorly translated as nonviolence, was rooted in spirituality. Of his pursuit of God, he said, "If I could persuade myself that I should find Him in a Himalayan cave, I would proceed there immediately. But I know that I cannot find Him apart from humanity."[7] The aim of his life would be to "see God," but that pursuit would lead him into politics. "For God,"

> The relationships that nurture the capacity for surprise and reverence are found by moving on one's own journey of faith and service.

he said, reversing centuries of tradition in a short sentence, "appears to you only in action."[8]

We are trained to think that when the discussion moves toward spirituality, it moves away from the physical. Gandhi— and I would argue Jesus and Muhammad and other proph- ets—showed us that the only way to sustain an integral, singular life is to work on what matters most to those who have the least. It is a journey in constant engagement with the *stuff* of life.

One could examine Gandhi's life to find a pattern of spiri- tual practices and rituals that made him integral, wholly consis- tent. Some of them, such as his commitment to abstinence in marriage, seem so radical as to be bizarre. He knew we needed not just a general theory about the world but rituals of passage, growth, lament, memory, and encouragement. Spinning wool and weaving his own simple clothes, cleaning out the latrines, eating no meat, and fasting before his campaigns were all ways of making the connections visible and vital. One of the great creative tasks of our time is to develop ways for us to be together amid the diversity and complexity of the boundary zones. If Gandhi needed rituals, perhaps we might also.

Amid the scale and complexity of boundary zones it is easy to overlook the basics of spiritual development. The very fact that we can speak of "traditions" means that many others have thought deeply about the path of life. It is possible to appreci- ate systematically the transformational potential of one's faith tradition. Doing so in the boundary-zone webs of relation- ships, it is also likely that it will open appreciation for others. One would hope this would happen in the places of higher education of our clergy, among our youth, and wherever faith- ful adults gather in study. Most syllabi are designed to rein- force the tribe and build up its walls with peculiar language justifying isolation and distance. Reading our Scriptures with boundary zone questions is like turning on the lights and see- ing all the words.

The path of spiritual development is intentionally moving along the boundary between holy and human. The strengths on which such a movement rests are social, not personal. In *Deeply Woven Roots* I described as one of the eight strengths of congregations the strength to pray. This includes the image that comes to mind for most: sitting in silence saying words in the hope they connect in some mysterious way to God. But it also includes the whole menu of ways we humans move to the boundary of the holy: dance, music, silence, presence, art, questions, inspired hopes, protest, candles, old and new symbols.

As Gandhi knew, we need rituals to help us find the path again and again. Ritual marks the paths toward, not away from, the complexity of the boundary zones. Indeed, ritual has a much larger bandwidth than mere rationality. It functions beyond, not beneath, logic. It includes physical/sensory triggers that connect us at depth and breadth. That is what the Lord's Supper does for Christians, involving all the senses, evoking all we know. Ritual includes patterns of participation that open up the space. As we saw at the beginning of the chapter, our institute participants create tapestries that are treated with reverence as instruments of knowing and transparency. We bring symbols of our lives and commitments and, as we name them publicly, we lay them on a common table lit only by a candle. As the table becomes cluttered, a coherence emerges that is the picture of a new "us." Symbols lead us beyond what we already know at the same time they remind us of what was known long before us.

Boundary leaders often imagine they are a few on the edges of the many. Ray and Anderson note in *Cultural Creatives* that there are fifty million adult Americans who are not conscious of themselves as a powerful cohort. They observe there is yet no "scaffolding" on which an identity could be visible; no language, gathering spaces, or rituals that help us mark our commonalities. When a group of public health and faith leaders gathered to explore how they might "deepen and accelerate" the convergence of faith and health, they wrote a

call to colleagues that included a vision of "strengthened congregations and other religious structures employing strengths
of language, symbols, rituals, and arts that continually humble,
nurture and ennoble our work."[9] A boundary spirituality is
finding symbols and language that people can recognize, calling to them at their depth and inviting them into the whole.

Boundary leadership is a constant cycling through the
process of comprehending and aligning the assets of the community system. There is not a final stage to be reached, at least
not in the imaginable lifespan of
anyone reading this edition of this
particular book. There is no stable
state in sight or even within the
reach of imagination. Even the
most optimistic boundary leader
knows that what will emerge
draws on a broader and more
complex menu of possibilities
than we can understand armed
with our partial knowledge and incomplete hopes. So our partial alignments will always be eclipsed by the next ones. Yet it
goes beyond that.

> **Boundary leadership is a
> constant cycling through
> the process of compre-
> hending and aligning the
> assets of the
> community system.**

Boundary leaders are marked by a restless faith that will
not give up. Larry James says that he believes more and more
in less and less. Me too. I believe that God is not done, and
that until God gives up, I am not going to either. I want to be
with people who believe that too. I find you everywhere I go
in the boundary zones with people who believe that too.

Drawn beyond our tribes by relationships that ask for and
make possible transformation, we move into the boundary
zones and find life amid the brokenness. We see our weaknesses with painful clarity, but also our strengths. Because we
are in webs of relationship that sustain, encourage, and transform, we find resilience and even power.

I began this book by asking what word we had for one
another. As is the way of the boundary places, any word really

worth sharing becomes flesh. The word that I see alive among us is our hope and blessing:

> God—as we know God by many names—
>> so loved the world
> That we are drawn into it.
> Do not be afraid
>> of that which God loves.
> Do not give up
>> on that which God loves.

Thanks

One would not think that a small book like this one would need so much help from so many. But I am whelmed over by the gifts I've received along the journey together. I live in daily debt to my colleagues of the Interfaith Health Program and the teams of our Institute for Public Health and Faith Collaborations, our Faith Health Consortium, and the many collaborations that define our life, not the least of which is my academic home at Emory University. I must name Mimi Kiser my Associate Director, Brad Gray, Jim Cochrane, and Fred Smith who teach me about leadership every time we meet. Wayne Merritt, friend and scholar, forced me toward clarity in the first drafts of this thinking while I was working on my DMin at the Interdenominational Theological Center. They must remain anonymous, but I am grateful to the original cohort of boundary leaders who submitted themselves to what must have seemed a long and strange interview.

I am indebted to Larry Pray, the writer and pastor who created the personal profiles in the book that bring my thinking to life. He knew what to listen for in the lives of those profiled partly because he thrives on the boundaries so much himself. As mentor for the Institute of Public Health and

Faith Collaborations, he has helped create the learning pathways that many others have followed.

Along with the amazing people at Fortress Press, Everett Hullum took the ten books in my mind and turned them into the one printed here. Patience is a rare virtue in the world of publishing, but my friend Michael West showed he has that one, along with the long list of others.

Some of the very best of our company of boundary leaders die far short of even the partial alignment they thought they could reach. This book was written with two such men often in my mind. Earl Shinhoster, former regional director of the NAACP, died at forty-nine as the car he was riding in blew a tire and hit a tree. Earl left a remarkable record of webs and influence; one of the brightest, toughest stars of the civil rights movement. Ironically, he was doing one of his more mundane boundary leader tasks, cruising along the interstate in a borrowed SUV to a speaking event nobody would remember a week later.

Jerry Gunnin, who died of ALS, was the opposite story from Earl: a member of the white power structure, senior vice president of the largest health care provider in Texas. But he was a boundary leader whose real authority rested on his integrity and hope for community that compelled even the toughest bottom-line board members to consider the possibilities of a different way, a community more whole and just.

Jerry and Earl died far short of the beloved community and they knew it. Both left a lot of wholeness un-emerged; left for other boundary leaders to pick up and weave together. If they had died peacefully at ninety-six, there would still have been a thousand hopes left for others to fulfill, which may be the best way to measure the value of a boundary leader. I hope they would recognize this book as part of their own legacy.

Anyone who knows me will sense how deeply this book is shaped by the nearly thirty years at Oakhurst Baptist Church. And I would hope they would recognize the powerful influence of the three women at the heart of my life: Karen, Lauren, and Kathryn.

Notes

Chapter 1: Come This Way

1. *The New International Webster's Pocket Dictionary of the English Language*, new rev. ed. (Naples, Fla.: Trident, 2001).

2. Scott Russell Sanders, *Writing from the Center* (Bloomington: Indiana University Press, 1997), 61.

Chapter 2: Boundary Zones

1. See: http://www.cdc.gov/omh/AboutUs/disparities.htm.

2. Jonathan Lomas, "Social Capital and Health: Implications for Public Health and Epidemiology," *Social Science and Medicine* 47, no. 9 (1988): 182.

3. National Center for Health Statistics, *Health, United States 2002*, Table 54.

4. Ibid.

5. Gary King and David R. Williams, "Race and Health: A Multidimensional Approach to African-American Health," in *Society and Health*, ed. Benjamin C. Amick III, Sol Levine, Alvin Tarlov, and Diane Chapman Walsh (New York: Oxford University Press, 1995), 107ff.

6. Fred Douglas Smith Jr., "Without a Vision: A Prophetic Christian Religious Education for Black Boys" (dissertation,

Emory University, Division of Religion, 1996).

7. King and Williams, "Race and Health," 107ff.

8. Camara Jones, "The Impact of Racism on Health," *Ethnicity and Disease* 12 (Winter 2002): s2–10.

9. Ibid., 10–13.

10. Jones describes these as institutional, "personally mediated" and internalized. I am using different nomenclature for the personally mediated level, but otherwise accept the definitions.

11. Paul Farmer and Didi Bertrand, "Hypocrisies of Development and the Health of the Haitian Poor," in *Dying for Growth: Global Inequality and the Health of the Poor,* ed. Jim Yong Kim, Joyce V. Millen, Alec Irwin, and John Gershman (Monroe, Maine: Common Courage, 2000), 87.

12. Ibid., 88.

13. Ibid.

14. Camara Jones, "The Impact of Racism on Health."

15. Smith, "Without a Vision," 15.

16. Ibid., 283.

17. Lyrics of "We've Come This Far By Faith" by Albert Goodson.

18. Lee G. Bolman and Terrance E. Deal, *Reframing Organizations: Artistry, Choice and Leadership,* 2nd ed. (San Francisco: Jossey-Bass, 1997), 15.

19. Ronald A. Heifetz, *Leadership Without Easy Answers* (Boston: Belknap, 1994).

20. See the Minnesota Department of Health Web site at http://www.health.state.mn.us/divs/chs/mhip/.

21. Bill McKibben, *The End of Nature* (New York: Anchor, 1990).

Chapter 3: Boundary Leaders

1. Paul H. Ray and Sherry Ruth Anderson, *The Cultural Creatives: How 50 Million People are Changing the World* (New York: Three Rivers, 2000); Laurent A. Parks Daloz, Cheryl H. Keen, James P. Keen, and Sharon Daloz Parks, *Common Fire* (Boston: Beacon, 1996).

2. Parks Daloz et al., *Common Fire*, 175.

3. Ray and Anderson, *Cultural Creatives*, 137.

4. Jim Young Kim, Joyce V. Millen, Alec Irwin, and John Gershman, eds., *Dying for Growth* (Monroe, Maine: Common Courage, 2000).

5. Paul Farmer, foreword to Kim et al., *Dying for Growth*, xiii.

6. Amartya Sen, foreword to *Pathologies of Power* by Paul Farmer (Berkeley: University of California Press, 2003), xvi.

7. Ibid., 5.

8. Parks Daloz et al., *Common Fire*, 3.

9. Ibid.

10. Unpublished paper by Gary Gunderson.

11. Parks Daloz et al., *Common Fire*, 73.

12. Ibid.

13. Malcom Gladwell, *The Tipping Point: How Little Things Can Make a Big Difference* (Boston: Little, Brown, 2000), 38–41.

14. Parks Daloz et al., *Common Fire*, 200.

15. Martin Luther King, Jr. "Nobel Prize Acceptance Speech" (Oslo, Norway, December 10, 1964).

16. Wendell Berry, "In Distrust of Movements," *Resurgence Magazine On-line* 198 (January-February 2000), http://resurgence.gn.apc.org/issues/berry198.htm.

17. Ibid.

18. Gunderson, *Deeply Woven Roots: Improving the Quality of Life in Your Community* (Minneapolis: Fortress Press, 1997), chapters 2–9.

Chapter 4: Webs of Transformation

1. Jim Wallace. "Micah's Challenge," in *Hearts and Minds*, for SOJO Mail, Spetember 24, 2003, http://www.sojo.net/index.cfm?action=sojomail.display&issue=030924#2.

2. Ibid.

3. James Cochrane, *Circles of Dignity: Community Wisdom and Theological Reflection* (Minneapolis: Fortress Press, 1998).

4. John Lewis, with Michael D'Orso, *Walking with the Wind* (New York: Simon & Schuster, 1998), 12–13.

5. Paul H. Ray and Sherry Ruth Anderson, *The Cultural Creatives: How 50 Million People Are Changing the World* (New York: Three Rivers Press, 2000).

6. Charles Jencks, *The Architecture of the Jumping Universe*, 2nd ed. (New York: Academy, 1997).

7. "Assets and Agency: Proceedings of the Africa Religious Health Assets Program Pietermaritzburg Colloquium," James Cochrane and Barbara Schmid, eds. (University of Cape Town, 2003).

8. Ray and Anderson, *Cultural Creatives*, 207.

Chapter 5: A Word for One Another

1. Walter Rauschenbusch, "Prayer for Tuberculosis Day" in *For God and the People: Prayers of the Social Awakening*. (1910; repr., Norwood, Pa.: Norwood Editions, 1978), 54.

2. Paul Farmer, *Pathologies of Power* (Berkeley: University of California Press, 2003), 255.

3. Rauschenbush, "Prayer for Tuberculosus Day."

4. William Sloane Coffin, *The Heart Is a Little to the Left* Boston: Univ. Press of New England, 1999), 4.

5. Colin M. Morris, *The Word and the words* (Nashville: Abingdon, 1975).

6. Jonathan Schell, *The Unconquerable World: Power, Nonviolence, and the Will of the People* (New York: Metropolitan, 2003), 106.

7. Ibid.

8. Ibid.

9. Paul H. Ray and Sherry Ruth Anderson, *The Cultural Creatives: How 50 Million People Are Changing the World* (New York: Three Rivers Press, 2000), 204.